PRAISE FOR ▌
NUMBERS 11, 22, AND 33

"Felicia's approach to numerology is insightful and fresh! Her knack for translating this complex, mystical language into relevant advice is why we chose her as the official numerologist for our website Astrostyle.com. Her readings have been life-changing for us personally and for our audience at large."
    —**Tali Edut**, owner of Astrostyle.com

"As a loyal and passionate reader of Felicia Bender's insights about numerology, I entirely trust her perceptions. True to form, Felicia has delicately handled the paradox of contextualizing advanced metaphysical concepts with inclusive and accessible language in *Master Numbers 11, 22, and 33*. I have a tighter, two-handed grip on the concept of Master numbers because of reading this book, which I recommend without reservation to anyone looking to advance their mastery of multidimensional knowledge."
    —**Colin Bedell**, astrologer with QueerCosmos.com and *Cosmopolitian*

"Felicia brilliantly helps us find comfort in numbers, by using them to show us the hidden meaning of our lives. And for that, I am so grateful."
    —**Erin Weed**, founder/CEO of Evoso, author, speaker, and TEDx Talks
    speaker coach

"Felicia Bender has done an excellent job with her book. I was blown away by her accuracy in describing my character traits. *Master Numbers 11, 22, and 33* brought me great clarity, wisdom, and peace. I began to understand my life and mission at a whole new level. What a relief! It immediately increased my confidence! Profound, insightful. Sheer wisdom. Extremely accurate."
    —**Joanna Garzilli**, America's Intuition Coach, author of *Big Miracles: The 11 Spiritual Rules for Ultimate Success*

Also by Felicia Bender:

Redesign Your Life:
Using Numerology to Create the Wildly Optimal You

MASTER NUMBERS
NUMBERS
11
22
33

THE ULTIMATE GUIDE

FELICIA BENDER, Ph.D.

FAB Enterprises Ltd./Felicia Bender
www.feliciabender.com

Cover design by the Book Designers
Interior design by Gus Yoo
Copy editing by Stephanie Gunning
Author photo by Jennifer Koskinen

Library of Congress Control Number PCN: 2018941760
ISBN 978-0-692-06835-9

Master Numbers 11 22 33/Felicia Bender —1st edition

To all those dedicated to embodying their highest calling

CONTENTS

PREFACE

One year I was in New York City at Christmastime. My friend and I were at an outdoor market where a wall had been made into a huge chalkboard that people could doodle and draw on. On this chalkboard was a drawing of an elf with the header: "What Do You Want for Christmas?" Three items were written on the Christmas wish list.

1. A sense of purpose
2. Sex
3. A money tree

Considering that a sense of purpose topped sex and a money tree, I found it an amusing yet powerful statement about what drives people overall. Everyone has a unique and powerful gift that we're born to give to benefit ourselves and the world. This gift involves a particular purpose or theme. We all have a burning desire to *know what that purpose is* so that we can actively focus on and pursue it with the most success and satisfaction.

I hold a doctorate in theater and have experience as an actor and a director, and I'm fascinated with human behavior and the emotional components that inform our actions and choices. When you get an acting role, most often you take time to analyze the script. Preparation through script analysis gives you a far better chance for a detailed and compelling performance. To play a role, an actor must decide—based on the script—what he feels is his character's "through line of action." In essence, this is the life purpose of the character that the actor will be immersed in. Knowing this through line, or purpose, the actor can give a successful performance in which the specificity of detail in every action, word, and silence is in alignment.

I feel that real people are driven to do the same thing. Only, our scripts are our lives and we are the leading players in our own dramas/comedies/musicals. The through lines of action we need to identify are our personal senses of purpose. Without them, we may feel rudderless.

In the past, in the pursuit of personal meaning I myself have gone the pinball route, bouncing and ricocheting as the "paddles" of life whacked my rear end from here to there and back again. I've spent more time than I care to admit waking up in tears—in despair about not wanting to waste another nanosecond without a clear sense of direction, passion, and purpose.

Yet, how was I to do better? Who or what could I trust to rub my nose in the truth of my being? I wanted to know: *Where does purpose live? How will I know when I find it?*

Some folks seem to be born with a sense of purpose. Most of us, however, struggle to name our purposes and act in ways that are aligned with them. From my seeking, I found a gem of a tool. It doesn't take a guru or years of initiation to make use of it. It's numerology. Numerology is the study of the art and science of numbers. The form of numerology I use comes from Pythagoras, the Greek mystic and mathematician who devised the Pythagorean theorem of geometry. This has something to do with right-angled triangles that you'll remember if you were paying attention in your grade-school math class, which I wasn't!

The basic concept of numerology is that numbers carry both a quantitative meaning—like counting one apple, two apples, and so on—and a frequency. Energetically, every number has a meaning and influence forming a vibrational matrix around it, if you will. Rather like the forces involved in cell phone reception, gravity, or the virtual cloud where we store our computer files, we don't have to understand it, or even believe it's there, for it to be operating.

Numerology uses your name and your birth date to formulate and reveal your vibrational matrix as an individual; and your numerological profile, or chart, indicates stages of development, cycles you'll experience in your life, and aspects of your personality. Many numerologists call our personal numbers a "blueprint" for life. You can think of yours as your individual life script, blueprint, roadmap, or mission statement. Or a through line for the play of your life.

How you interpret the numbers is as much an art as a science. For me, numerology answers the question "What am I supposed to be doing?" in a way that offers a definitive through line of action. What I've also figured out is that sometimes part of a life's purpose is the urgent seeking of the life's purpose. A cruel joke? And yet—there it is.

Furthermore, after years of study and analyzing thousands of people's numerology charts my primary takeaway is this: Whatever each of us came here to do is always going to be the most difficult thing for us to do. That's why it takes a lifetime to align with it.

This means that whatever each of us is here to do cannot be accomplished in a weekend workshop. The more we flounder around without taking the time, effort, and energy to do our "script analysis," the sloppier and less effective our "performance" will be.

Did you ever see that old TV game show called *Wipeout*? It was a show where contestants would compete for money to take the shortest amount of time getting through a horrendous monstrosity of a moving obstacle course. Despite the hardship, you didn't see the contestants who entered the obstacle course participating like many of us participate in our daily lives—acting depressed, pissed off, or bored. No. Oh no! These people looked at the giant obstacle course that was guaranteed to beat the living daylights out of them, and they were jumping up and down with enthusiasm, so *psyched* to give it a go.

Life is a lot like a *Wipeout* obstacle course, and yet most of us don't approach it as those contestants did! We grumble and wonder *Why me?* because we think it should be fair, different, better, easier, and simpler—to the point where we are always pushing back on the way life is unfolding for us. Numerology provides you with a framework to understand what your obstacle course may look like, so you can get amped up and ready yourself to tackle it head on.

What numerology had to tell me about myself was what I'd always known inside, deep down to the crevices of my being. Living in the world tends to beat the real you out of you. Although I felt beaten down in the past, once I could see myself through the lens of numerology, I experienced a massive turnaround in the way I position myself in the world. This information changed the way I think about everything: the purpose and meaning of life, work, and relationships—*all of it*. Numerology has reframed my engagement with virtually everything from the ground up.

In real-world terms, with this tool I could identify the "Real Me" and see where I was taking detours from acting upon it. The idea that there is profound meaning and order in the chaos we call our lives was something I could hold on to.

Since then, I have found that other people click into insights drawn from their numerology charts and resonate similarly with the information in a way that feels to them as if some of the lost puzzle pieces of their lives have been dug out from a dark place under the bed, extracted from the dust bunnies, and put back on the table and reassembled.

Understand that living with authenticity and a clear sense of purpose isn't easy. In fact, it's hard. The path is mutable. Progress is incremental. What we're here to accomplish will be the ultimate challenge—in a good way. You can expect to feel both exaltedly ecstatic and strangely uncomfortable when you're aligning with your correct through line of action. People won't necessarily agree with you. You'll face your biggest fears again and again. You'll sometimes be your own saboteur. You may on occasion feel starved for a shot of validation and more profound meaning, understanding, and perspective about what you're doing and why you're doing it. Purpose mutates, goes through stages of development and completion, and yet grows like a well-tended garden when given the proper care and maintenance.

While it may be easy to use metaphors drawn from the theater and gardening, I find that because we're in an extraordinarily volatile time in the world people are seeking deeper meaning in a way that they haven't in the past. Our problems feel more immediate and immense than ever before. For anyone who's interested in metaphysics or anything on the spiritual or esoteric realm, it's not news that we're going through significant transitions in different spheres, from political conflicts to destructive weather patterns and other forms of international crises. Information about cosmic energy shifts, cycles of transition, and the awakening of planetary consciousness is available through astrology, numerology, science, and other outlets of information. Even with this information at hand, people are hungry for solutions for the world's more prominent problems and for their personal problems. Those who are awake spiritually are intensely aware that they have an essential role to play in this transitional period.

So why have I chosen to write a book on the Master numbers 11, 22, and 33? In my professional numerology practice, I've found that I attract many clients who have Master numbers in their charts. I've done consultations for a vast number of individuals who are struggling to find a way to understand and manage the high-powered energy of the Master numbers and to make sense of the energy in their daily lives. It's for all of you—and you know who you are—that this book has come to fruition. I know that the demands the Master numbers place on you can feel disconcerting and relentless. This book is designed to offer you practical guidance as you navigate the different stages of your life as you hone your high-level skills and talents and embrace your intense journey.

Coming to terms with the calling of a Master number will allow you to move forward with an absolute sense of yourself, no matter how convoluted everything around you might seem. Embracing your numbers is not magic or woo-woo; it's about understanding yourself on a deep level. It's about inviting yourself to engage with the cycles in your life in a productive way rather than expecting to be able to follow a linear path that doesn't exist.

If the TV program *Wipeout* is a fair reflection or metaphor for the normal life, then think about the trajectory for those with Master numbers as being participants on a next-level game show, such as *Ultimate Ninja Warrior*. The ironic thing is that if you have Master numbers in your numerology profile, you initially *thought* you signed up for *Wipeout* and then somehow ended up on the set for *Ultimate Ninja Warrior* even though you have no idea how you got there.

"Proper preparation prevents poor performance" is an excellent mantra for an actor. You can also apply this truism to your life in general. Find your through line of action. Show up for your performance. Have fun. Make it count. It's imperative—now more than ever—that if you have one or more Master numbers in your chart you come to terms with your calling and begin to make the contribution to the world that you were born to make. Only by understanding the complexity and the beauty of your mission can you fully step into your power.

INTRODUCTION

Master numbers hold an infinite fascination for those who resonate with numerology. If you have a Master number—or more than one Master number—in your numerology chart, you might want to know how to deal with it from day to day. Most people *want* to have Master numbers (or a Master number) in their charts. Do you feel this way? And if you do, why? Glutton for punishment, perhaps?

This book will introduce you to the Master numbers 11, 22, and 33, explaining what they are and how to work with the mission they bring with them. I'm offering you an immersive, practical, and user-friendly approach to managing and aligning successfully with the powerful energy inherent to Master numbers.

In writing this book, I'm taking a bit of an academic approach because I wasn't born knowing numerology and I'm betting you weren't either. I have studied it, put it into practice, and I'm still learning, learning, learning. Therefore, I'll offer you different ideas, thoughts, and approaches to help you wrap your head around what the Master numbers bring to the game of life. I'll attempt to expose you to different schools of thought and offer some observations from other numerologists about key elements of the Master numbers 11, 22, and 33.

My approach is primarily related to how to use numerological information in the most user-friendly, everyday way. I think we all want to know: How do we recognize the issues related to having one or more Master numbers in our own charts or in the charts of the people we know and care for? How can we apply this knowledge to feel as though we're doing what we're "supposed" to be doing with this elevated sense of purpose? What tendencies and obstacles are commonly related to the Master numbers?

Many numerologists emphasize the esoteric meaning and influence of the Master numbers and suggest that the higher frequency contained in—and disseminated by—the Master numbers activates higher levels of evolution within human consciousness. While some Master numbers are currently activated and at work within our contemporary world, more Master numbers will be activated in the future. We are part of a continuous evolutionary process.

Fundamentally, the repetition of any number magnifies—indeed, doubles—the influence and intensity of that number. Some numerologists, however, assert that there are only three true Master numbers—the ones we are discussing: 11, 22, and 33. Their emphasis on these three Master numbers doesn't diminish the fact that other repeating numbers have significant power. Their argument is that other repeating numbers aren't "pure" or aren't yet activated within the construct of an individual numerology profile. For instance, I have worked with a young client in her teens who has a 44/8 Life Path number. Yet that is not common.

It's often thought that people with Master numbers in their charts are older souls who have knowledge and information from former lifetimes available to them. Some feel that those with Master vibrations are continuing work they started during previous incarnations. While that might sound somewhat special and lofty, it doesn't equate to happiness or having an easy life. Those with Master numbers often experience severe challenges throughout their lives.

So, while there are esoteric and "out there" ways to understand the meaning and calling of the Master numbers, it's important and more helpful to know how to manage the day-to-day intensity, challenges, and potentials of these numbers. How can we cope with and balance the Master energy? How can we take it in and act upon it in theory and in practice?

While we'll go through the ways to calculate the basics of a numerology chart, also know that there are many apps that can calculate a full chart for you. Among professional and semiprofessional numerologists, the most widely used and recommended software programs are from Hans Decoz and Matthew Goodwin. I turn to Decoz as the final word on the most accepted or proper way to calculate a chart. For links to the software program and mobile apps I recommend, visit my website, www.FeliciaBender.com/Resources. You must find the app or software program that works best for you and do your homework to make sure the way it calculates your numbers is the way you feel is correct. Given that you're particularly concerned with the Master numbers, it's in your best interest to double check any 2, 4, or 6 that shows up to see if it calculates as a Master number using a different style of calculation. Most software will not indicate a Master number 33.

Understand that having Master numbers in a chart or during a cycle of your life will undoubtedly intensify and possibly complicate your experience. Even so, we can't say that having a "regular" chart would promise less intensity or smoother sailing. Enrolling in this school we call life is never without incident. Remember that everyone is here for a reason and has a soul contract to fulfill and a purpose to act upon. Everyone also has the gift and the responsibility of free will. We have the choice as to how we carry out our mission.

PART ONE

BREAKING
IT
DOWN

CHAPTER 1

WHAT ARE MASTER NUMBERS?

In numerology, double-digit numbers that repeat the same number—such as 11, 22, 33—are considered Master numbers. Some numerologists observe only the 11 and the 22 when they work with core numbers in your chart. But others, like me, also work with the 33. As mentioned in the Introduction, all repeating numbers can be considered Master numbers. It's just that the ones that show up in a numerology chart are the 11, 22, and 33. The numbers 44, 55, 66, 77, 88, and 99 therefore don't need to be discussed within the context of interpreting a contemporary numerology chart.

You may also be interested to know that many numerologists never reduce Master numbers to one-digit numbers. For them, an 11 is always 11, a 22 is always 22, and a 33 is always 33.

Other numerologists indicate the Master number by writing it this way: 11/2, 22/4, and 33/6 because we are interested in how the energy of the final digit affects the chart. It's up to you to feel out what works best and what feels right to you. I like the nuance of this approach.

Also note that many numerologists never reduce a Master number when it's *used in a calculation*. Therefore, an 11 remains an 11, not a 2. The 22 is 22, not a 4. And a 33 is always 33, never 6. Ultimately, it will be up to you to determine how you prefer to approach the calculations.

The power of a Master number resides in its inherent polarity. With the 11/2, the repeated number 1 can be considered masculine energy (doubled) that is being added to the number 2, which embodies feminine energy. Therefore, the energy matrix of the 11/2 Master number holds limitless power, with the potential of the convergence of the most optimal qualities of masculine and feminine energy.

The Master number 22/4 combines the feminine 2 (doubled), which indicates significant intuition capacity, with the structured number 4, which indicates rationality.

And the Master number 33/6 is a collision of the emotionally expressive and creative 3 (doubled) with the teaching, service, and caregiving of the 6. We might look at the Master numbers as rungs on a ladder, where each number represents a step toward spiritual enlightenment. From the 11, we gain spiritual illumination; from the 22, we bring heaven down to earth and build something in the material world: and the 33 is a culmination of these two steps. This brings higher consciousness to others in the form of love, service, teaching, and vision.

CHAPTER 2

CORE ELEMENTS OF NUMEROLOGY

YOUR LIFE PATH NUMBER

Calculated by adding together the birth date.
Day + Month + Year

Your Life Path number indicates your mission or overall purpose. This is what you're learning, mastering, and evolving into overall in this lifetime. In Chapter 3, "Getting Started on Your Chart," you will learn the three most common ways to calculate your Life Path number. When your Life Path number is a Master number, it has a powerful impact on your life. It signifies that you'll have specific innate gifts and talents (depending on which Master number it is) and more distinct or heightened challenges on the road to mastering your Life Path purpose.

The natural gifts of the Master number will affect you whenever it shows up in your chart. But when it's your Life Path number, it's the *driving* force in your life. So, plan to get to know its victories and challenges intimately. The demands of a Master Life Path number will affect you very directly, as this is your life's work.

YOUR DESTINY OR EXPRESSION NUMBER

Calculated by adding together all the letters of the full name as it appears on the birth certificate.

Your Destiny or Expression number points to the way you'll express your life purpose as indicated by your Life Path number. When a Master number shows up here, it's a great indicator of the type of work or career that is best for you. This number indicates the "flavor" of how, or the manner in which you'll go about, achieving your life's purpose.

For example, let's say you have a 3 Life Path number and an 11/2 Destiny or Expression number. Given what you know about these numbers, how would you guess or interpret the significance of this combination? I would say that a person with this combination has the potential to have focal points on emotional sensitivity perhaps with issues revolving around a weakness in following through on projects or ideas. This combination can also result in someone working in counseling, entertainment, or another profession where his or her performance and communication skills primarily revolve around helping and healing others on some level.

The wildcard in this combination is the double 1 of the 11. This energy amplifies the creativity of the already creative 3, and yet would make it a challenge for you to speak up for yourself.

You'll see that when the Master number shows up in your chart as the Destiny or Expression number, it impacts the way in which you go about doing what you do. It also gives you a hint as to what your overall destiny might be and guides how you engage on this level.

YOUR SOUL URGE OR HEART'S DESIRE NUMBER

Calculated by adding together all the vowels in the full name as it appears on the birth certificate.

Your Soul Urge number reveals what you want and need deep down on a soul level to feel content and satisfied. When a Master number shows up here in your chart, the interpretation can be more elusive. A soul urge is a deep-seated desire for a certain type of opportunity—and yet it may get sublimated or buried for periods of time. Even so, an internal pressure always comes to you, like a soft voice, which is your heart's desire attempting to be heard.

Underneath it all, you have a Master element to you that perhaps is perplexing, depending on how it merges and converges with the rest of your core numbers. Just know that this is alive and well—even if it feels a bit dormant or hard to reach sometimes. Some people always follow their hearts, and in this instance, perhaps having a Master Soul Urge number means that you're a person who feels more connected with this aspect of yourself and you find that this is a powerful influence on you overall.

Letters have numerical correspondences.

Vowels are highlighted.

1	2	3	4	5	6	7	8	9
A	B	C	D	E	F	G	H	I
J	K	L	M	N	O	P	Q	R
S	T	U	V	W	X	Y	Z	

How you work with the letter Y is perhaps the most subjective of all the numerological calculations when you're determining your Soul Urge number. There is occasionally a debate among grammarians about whether the letter W counts as a vowel—but I have never seen it counted as such by numerologists. The Y is more controversial.

In her book *Numerology*, Juno Jordan says this about calculating the Soul Urge number, which she calls the Heart number or Heart's Desire number.

In figuring the Heart Number use only the vowels: A, E, I, O, U. The W and Y are sometimes vowels but are not correctly used in figuring the inner or soul urge. The Heart's Desire is found from the soft lip-sounds of song and harmony. The W is a restless, difficult, and testing influence and not part of the inner nature. The Y is a crossroads, mystical, occult, wise, separate, and reserved, but very often stands for the unknown and what is to come. Its influence and power in the life of the individual or in your life is shown in the lesson Points of Intensification. It does not enter into the Heart's Desire. Some names have no other vowel but Y. This indicates a spiritual development being made but not fully developed in this lifetime.[1]

Hans Decoz offers this mode of thought and practice.

The letter Y is inherently vacillating in its nature and usage, and consequently is sometimes a vowel, sometimes a consonant, depending upon how it is used in the name. When determining if the Y is a vowel or a consonant in a numerology chart, the basic rule is this: When the letter serves as a vowel, and in fact sounds like one, it is a vowel. The same is true when the Y serves as the only vowel in the syllable. Examples of both of these cases are such names as Lynn, Yvonne, Mary, Betty, Elly, and Bryan. However, if the Y does not provide a separate vowel sound, as when it is coupled with another vowel, it is considered a consonant. In names such as Maloney or Murray, the Y is a consonant, because the vowel sound depends upon the long E in Maloney and the long A in Murray. In general, the Y is a consonant when the syllable already has a vowel. Also, the Y is considered a consonant when it is used in place of the soft J sound, such as in the name Yolanda or Yoda. In the names Bryan and Wyatt, the Y is a vowel, because it provides the only vowel sound for the first syllable of both names. For both of these names, the letter A is part of the second syllable, and therefore does not influence the nature of the Y.[2]

On the Widening Horizons software program, the message that shows up when the name contains a Y is:

This name has the letter Y in it. The Y is a vowel if it follows A, E, I, O, or U and sounds as one sound (as in Hayes) or there is no other vowel in the syllable (as in Ken-ne-dy) or it is pronounced as a vowel (as in Yves). Otherwise it is a consonant.

It won't surprise you at this point to know that other numerologists feel that the Y is always considered a vowel no matter what. Are you confused yet? The point is, I can tell you what I think is true, but you must eventually come to terms with your own conception of the calculations.

YOUR PERSONALITY NUMBER

Calculated by adding together all the consonants in the full name as it appears on the birth certificate.

Your Personality number indicates how others perceive you. It's indicative of how you appear to others in the outer world. It is the personality projected to the external world. If a Master number shows up here, chances are that the world perceives you as someone with powerful potential. Their perspective will depend on you individually and how your Master energy is manifesting for you. For number-to-letter correspondences, see the unshaded letters in the box on page 25.

YOUR BIRTHDAY NUMBER

The day you were born.

Your Birthday number is a vital indicator of a secondary gift you possess that is yours to give to yourself and the world. It's also often where you feel most comfortable or where you might more fully identify yourself. You're being asked to take the characteristics you develop with this number and integrate it to enhance your individual and unique spin on your Life Path mission. If you carry a Master number as your Birthday number, you have a lot of power at your disposal. You're being asked to embody the most positive elements of the Master number and allow it to integrate into, and inform your Life Path purpose.

YOUR MATURITY OR ACHIEVEMENT NUMBER

Calculated by adding together the Life Path number and the Destiny or Expression number.

Your Maturity or Achievement number is the combination of your Life Path number and your Destiny or Expression number, which indicates your ultimate destiny at the end of your life. If a Master number shows up here, don't count on having a low-key retirement! You're pointed in the direction of spiritual attainment.

Many people have charts overflowing with Master numbers and/or Karmic numbers (see definition below). It's not uncommon to see charts where a person can be working with repeating Master numbers or a combination of Master numbers and Karmic numbers.

KARMIC NUMBERS

When you see a 13, 14, 16, or 19 in your numerology chart, it's a *Karmic number.* People usually cringe when they see one or more of these types of numbers in a chart because they imagine that this means that they've somehow done something wrong in this lifetime. This isn't the case! Karmic numbers are specific indicators that there have been infractions of some kind in one or more of your past lives—so if you can discern what the infractions were, this knowledge could be amazingly powerful in helping you right the energy imbalance and create harmony.

Having a Karmic number in your chart is a way to understand why you're experiencing intense issues in certain key areas of your life. Identifying one can help you to appreciate your progress on a spiritual level. If you've been working hard at paying your Karmic debt, eventually you will be able to look at yourself and say: "Wow, I used to have a lot of problems in this area and yet I don't anymore. I've really come to terms with that aspect of my life or my behavior."

Also know that we're all experiencing a current lifetime that's an accumulation of karma from past lives, therefore any numerology chart can provide interesting insight into what karma may be indicated overall. Yet in numerology, when we have any of the numbers 13, 14, 16, or 19 in our chart, it provides specific information as to the nature of the debt we're paying back now.

Knowing the key elements of a karmic lesson or debt offers specific points of reference for you to continue to work with the issues successfully and continue to balance your karma.

Numerologists sometimes will refer to a Karmic number as a Testing number, a Warning number, or a Hidden number.

THE KARMIC NUMBER 13/4 AS IT RELATES TO MASTER NUMBER 22/4

Often the number 4 shows up either as a Master 22/4 or a Karmic 13/4—depending on the method of calculation—particularly when calculating your Life Path number. It's important to understand how the 22/4 might show up if you have a 4 in your chart and how you might understand the colliding, yet different issues related to the Master number versus the Karmic number. It's always up to you to decide which kind of number a number is—Karmic or Master?

For instance, medical intuitive Caroline Myss' Life Path number calculated one way is a Master 22/4. Calculated another way it is a Karmic 13/4.

Her birthdate is: December 2, 1952.

If you add the proper way (month/day/year)—meaning, as Hans Decoz and some other numerologists would greatly recommend—the calculation looks like this.

December is 12 and $1 + 2 = 3$
The day is 2
The year is $1 + 9 + 5 + 2 = 17$ and $1 + 7 = 8$

Then add 3 + 2 + 8 = 13 and 13/4 is a Karmic number.

If you take Myss' birthdate and add the long way (as Dan Millman and other numerologists would recommend), then it goes like this:

1 + 2 + 2 + 1 + 9 + 5 + 2 = 22

And 22 is a Master number—22/4

Either way you add up Myss' numbers, I would emphasize that she has "checked in" to master the most positive elements of the number 4.

There's much to be said about each Karmic number, yet for our purposes we will only look at 13/4, because it's the only one that has the potential to interplay with Master number 22/4.

If you have a Karmic 13/4 as one of your core numbers, understand that you're now paying back a debt for past abuses where carrying your share of the workload and your share of responsibility was seriously shirked. Remember that the number 1 (in 13) indicates selfishness. The number 3 in the 13/4 represents creative energy, expression, and joyfulness that turned into superficiality, irresponsibility, and using words to hurt others during a previous lifetime. As a Karmic number, the 13 indicates that you'll be required to exert some concerted effort and dig in with some hard work on a consistent basis in your life.

Hard work and steadily meeting your goals will be an ongoing requirement in this lifetime and much of the time it will feel difficult and "unfair." The 13/4 tells you that you're being asked to monitor and master the *art of positive expression*—and you can understand that as thinking before you speak, not being critical and judgmental, and using your words to support and uplift others rather than to tear them down. One of the tasks indicated with the 13/4 has to do with the mastery of emotional self-expression and emotional sensitivity. You might say that the Karmic 13/4 requires that you work diligently to bring a heightened level of precision to all of your communication.

If you have the 13/4 as one of your core numbers, you'll most likely act upon the more destructive tendencies of the number 4 until the lessons have been understood, acknowledged, acted upon, and mastered. Understand that—overall—you're being tested to really, truly, deeply master and embody the positive elements of the number 4. It's like you're being asked to become the "poster child" for the positive elements of the number 4—including working diligently to obtain goals, creating a systematic way of life, working with and around limitation, and creating a stable and secure existence for yourself and others.

The trick is that it won't be easy. You'll get a throw down in the realm of the lessons of the number 4 and you'll be called upon to really work with it in a conscious and consistent manner. The path of the number 4 is one of slow and steady process and progress. It's tenacious and hardworking, loyal and steady, intelligent, and able to build something of lasting value with systems and structures that the 4 is gifted at producing.

Add the 13 on top of it and it might then become apparent why you might feel done in or exhausted—and that no matter how much effort you exert, others always seem to come out ahead of you. Often the Karmic 13/4 brings heightened levels of the oppositional pull of the number 4, which might show up as the avoidance of responsibility, a lack of ability to set and follow through with goals, and generally finding yourself unable to put forth the concerted effort it takes to create stability in your life. With the 13/4, you're also being required to develop a strong sense of discipline and use systems and order in all practical matters throughout your life. Understand that people who have the 13/4 as one of their core numbers will most likely act upon the more destructive tendencies of the number 4 until the lessons have been understood, acknowledged, acted upon, and mastered. Some of the negative or challenging traits that must be grappled with are:

A Severe Sense of Limitation. One of the issues that can make an appearance when you're working with the Karmic 13/4 is in the realm of blame. The default for the difficulties the 13/4 experiences can be pushed over into blaming others (or everything—government, your family, your employer) for the limitations you experience. This can express as very dogmatic viewpoints or obsessive levels of rigidity. The 4 is always challenged with having a rather know-it-all approach to life and when the 13/4 is present, this can be even more of an obstacle.

Distorted Expression. Remember that infractions from a prior lifetime resided in distorted expression and so this time around, you'll be on a very short leash insofar as the demand that you express and communicate with the utmost clarity, fairness, and compassion. Therefore, there can be tendencies toward negative expression, like constant complaining—and hurting others with gossip or sarcasm. There can be a certain level of behaving in an obstinate fashion—digging your heels in and not moving or being open to new information or negotiation. Often the 13/4 can bring a level of close-mindedness that guarantees frustration and feelings of limitation.

The Anti-4. The oppositional pull presents itself with great strength when you're working with the Karmic 13/4. Therefore, you can be met with issues related to the opposite of your purpose. So rather than forging ahead with clearly defined goals and meeting those goals with diligence and concerted effort, you can instead ramble around without a rudder and never devote yourself to taking charge of your life or to building the security you would ultimately thrive upon. Rather than being a foundation builder and systems person, you lack the drive or focus to do what needs to be done. Instead of taking the path of the one who gets 'er done, you default into laziness and in many ways won't devote yourself to settling in for the long haul. You can lack clear direction and find it baffling and frustrating that you aren't feeling a sense of purpose and fulfillment. Often this manifests as pushing off responsibility to others while feeling a strong sense of entitlement.

I once had a client who scheduled a session, yet he emphasized the fact that he couldn't show up earlier than 1 P.M. because he routinely slept until at least noon. He was twenty-nine-years old and enrolled in a spiritually based school and yet he admitted that he habitually used marijuana and wasn't excelling with his classwork or any other part of his life. When I asked him why he scheduled an appointment to see me, he heaved a deep sigh and said: "I just don't think I'm living up to my potential." To which I observed that he wasn't! He was a 13/4 Life Path, or a 22/4 Life Path, depending on how you calculate, and this snippet of our conversation is a good illustration of tendencies someone working with this number might manifest. The great thing about it is that he knew he wasn't doing what he needed to be doing and was seeking support to see how he might understand it and change it.

If this description just doesn't sound anything like you or who you think you are, then potentially you're at a stage of development and maturity in your life—and have been working diligently on your own personal growth and evolution—where you're more in alignment with the constructive elements of the number 4. If that describes you, then hats off to you! You've been doing your work. It never hurts to give yourself a pat on the back for a job well done.

The gift you're given by knowing that you have a karmic debt to pay is this: Rather than feeling victimized, you can see this is something that you brought on yourself—despite the fact that you can't remember it. Not in a shameful way, rather in a mindful way where you simply take responsibility for yourself and for your actions and inactions. If you exert the energy and commitment to working in the positive realm of the number 4, then you'll reap the benefits. The karmic debt can feel rather grueling and somewhat unfair. You must go through an intense reconstruction or regeneration process to come to terms with and clear your karmic slate.

Working with the Karmic number 13/4 intensifies the issues that relate to the number 4. It's not easy. It requires concerted effort and focused commitment. It's testing you and requiring that you rewire the way you work with limitation, process, systems building, hard work, and setting foundations in life. It demands that you clarify and clean up the way you express yourself on every level. The destructive path might feel more comfortable since you've been there, done that. This time, you're being asked to extract yourself from riding in that same rut in the road—you're required to create a new way of working with these themes that have positive results for you and everyone around you.

GETTING STARTED ON YOUR CHART

CHAPTER 3

To start, if you calculate your Life Path number and get an 11, 22, or 33 before you reduce it to the 2, 4, or 6, you have a Master number as your Life Path number. As previously mentioned, you can also experience Master numbers in other aspects of your chart, such as the Destiny number, the Soul Urge number, the Maturity number, the Personality number, and so on.

Not to mention that you can also have Master numbers for calculations of Personal Year cycles, Pinnacles, and other cycles. If you find Master numbers anywhere in your chart, you'll benefit from learning more about what this could mean for you. Let's begin with the Life Path number.

Understand also that there are several ways to calculate the Life Path number. I was taught that the proper way is to add the month/day/year separately and then add the three single-digit numbers together (month/day/year). Here's an example.

Birthdate: February 2, 1987
February = 2
Day = 2
Year = 1987
1 + 9 + 8 + 7 = 25
Keep adding 2 + 5 = 7
Add the month, day, year: 2 + 2 + 7 = 11
11 is a Master number
It's sometimes written this way: 11/2

Let's use this same birthdate and show the other two ways to add it up.

First, you can add the entire birthdate together like one long addition problem: 2 + 2 + 1 + 9 + 8 + 7 = 29.

Keep adding: 2 + 9 = 11.

Although this is a rarely suggested way to calculate, you can also do it this way:

$$\begin{array}{r} 2 \\ 2 \\ + \ 1987 \\ \hline = 1991 \end{array}$$

This becomes: 1 + 9 + 9 + 1 = 20
Which then reduces to: 20 = 2 + 0 = 2

In this case, the Master number 11/2 does not show up.

The equation above is an example of how the 11 can show up as a Life Path number in some ways of calculation while it doesn't show up in others. Again, it's up to you as to how you decide to calculate your numbers. Some numerologists would say that a Master number is only valid when adding the "proper" way (by first reducing day/month/year and then adding the single-digit numbers together), while others will assert that adding the long way is also valid.

And remember, some numerologists *never reduce a Master number under any circumstances.* For example, if you were of the school of thought that we should never reduce Master numbers, and your birthday was November 22, 1988, you might calculate the Life Path number like this:

November = 11

$22 = 22$

$1988 = 1 + 9 + 8 + 8 = 26$

$2 + 6 = 8$

$11 + 22 + 8 = 41; 4 + 1 = 5$

Rather than: $11 = 1 + 1 = 2$

$22 = 2 + 2 = 4$

$1988 = 1 + 9 + 8 + 8 = 26$

$2 + 6 = 8$

$2 + 4 + 8 = 14; 1 + 4 = 5$

The result is the same, yet the two-digit number before you reduce to the one-digit number will be different. It depends on how detailed and nuanced you plan to get with your analysis as to how you prefer to read these details.

If we stay with this example, you can see what I mean.

$11 = 1 + 1 = 2$

$22 = 2 + 2 = 4$

$1988 = 1 + 9 + 8 + 8 = 26$ and $2 + 6 = 8$

$2 + 4 + 8 = 14/5$ and 14/5 is a Karmic number (see page 28).

The Life Path would be a Karmic 14/5 rather than 41 before reducing to a 5. Again, it's up to you to do your research and feel out how you feel it should operate.

CHAPTER 4

YOUR NAME AND MASTER NUMBERS

Let's look at how a Master number might show up when using your name rather than your date of birth. For this example, we'll calculate the Expression or Destiny number. For this number, you'll translate all the letters in the name into numbers (see chart) and add it together. The Soul Urge and the Personality numbers also use the letters of the name, yet the Soul Urge calculation uses only the vowels and the Personality calculation uses only the consonants. You use the same basic calculation, but there's a different way of processing it.

For this example, let's calculate the Destiny or Expression number for comedian Jerry Seinfeld. His full name is Jerome Allen Seinfeld.

I	2	3	4	5	6	7	8	9
A	B	C	D	E	F	G	H	I
J	K	L	M	N	O	P	Q	R
S	T	U	V	W	X	Y	Z	

Using the chart, we can see that Jerome translates into a 1, 5, 9, 6, 4 and 5, which added together equal 30. Then we take the 30 and keep adding the two digits. So, 3 + 0 = 3.

We do the same for both ALLEN and SEINFELD. Allen adds to an 8 and Seinfeld to an 11. Remember, many numerologists never reduce a Master number. If this is your system, the 11 remains an 11. If not, you continue reducing: 1 + 1 = 2.

All together, we add 3 (Jerome) + 8 (Allen) + 11 (Seinfeld) = 22.

With this calculation, Jerry Seinfeld has a 22/4 Destiny or Expression number.

If you're of the school of thought that reduces a Master number, then the calculation changes: 3 (Jerome) + 8 (Allen) + 2 (Seinfeld) = 13 (13 is a Karmic number), and then reduce those two digits further: 1 + 3 = 4.

The point of this illustration is to make you aware that if you do get a 2, 4, or 6 you should always calculate both ways to see if a Master number is present. It does make a difference.

Most numerologists assert that the original name holds permanent potency and will always be the foundational energetic matrix that each of us works with throughout our lives. A name change obviously alters the energy that we carry and the longer that new name represents us, the more infused that power and mission become in our lives. It's no wonder why many entertainers change their names—that name change brings in a different vibe that can help them achieve greater success.

It's also no wonder that women often experience a bit of a personality quandary periodically given that they often change their names in their lives through marriage, divorce, and by choice. Not to say that women marry and divorce more frequently than men, yet women are the ones who traditionally change the last name while men keep their names throughout their lives no matter what their marital status might be. Of course, there are exceptions to this, yet this remains our overarching cultural practice.

Keep this important element in mind: In numerology, you must use the name you were given at birth, as written on your birth certificate. Even if there is a misspelling, that's the spelling used for the calculation. If you were adopted, use the original name given on your birth certificate. Of course, you'll run the chart for the name change, yet numerologically speaking the original name you were given is your foundational energetic matrix for this lifetime. You must use the whole name, even if you don't like it.

If you have more than one middle name, use all the names as they appear on your birth certificate.

If you're a Junior, a Second, or a Third, leave those distinctions out of the equation.

These are the basic rules when using Pythagorean numerology. Other forms of numerology—including, but not limited to Chaldean numerology—have different modes of thinking. We're using the Pythagorean system here. Those are the basic rules for any calculation dealing with your name.

To get technical about it, I find that when the Master number doesn't show up with the first way of adding (the proper way), you can continue to add it up using the other two calculations—whether this is for a number derived from the date of birth or the name. If it shows up in only one calculation, you can view the energy of the Master number as "optional." Again, many numerologists would argue that the only time a Master number is a Master number is when it shows up when—and only when—it appears when calculated a certain way.

You might think of it this way: It's as though you were on the "other side" and coming up with a mission you wanted to pursue and learn about during this lifetime. At that time, you thought: "Hey, I can do that Master thing!" And yet you also thought: "What if it's too much for me?" So, at that point it's as though your soul gave you a choice. You opted to endow yourself with a hidden Master number so that you could make the decision to go for the gusto if you wanted once you found yourself inhabiting this body on Planet Earth. You also gave yourself an out—the *out* being that you could make the determination to instead work with the energy related to the single number. So, while you'll continue to feel some internal burn related to the Master number, you can opt for the lower octave, so to speak, and be just fine.

Some numerologists feel this way about the Master numbers overall. They feel that that someone can opt for the lower vibration of the single-digit number if the Master vibration feels too intense or overwhelming. Many numerologists feel that the Master number is the Master number and can only be counted as such when it comes up in the proper Pythagorean way of calculation. Again, I'm presenting the primary options that different schools of thought offer you.

Just realize that the Master number brings with it an intensity that's undeniable. It's generally observed that the Master numbers bring a higher spiritual purpose, no matter how you might define that. The Master numbers carry a higher frequency and vibratory influence. Energetically speaking, they're always pushing you. You're going to feel high-strung emotions mixed with a certain level of anxiety when you're working with a Master number—particularly when it shows up as your Life Path or another of your core numbers.

You're going to feel a constant push and pull to be more and do better, often to the point of distraction. You might also notice that you have high expectations for yourself, even when others can't see how much pressure is building up inside of you. Or should we say, especially when others can't see that you feel anxious 24/7.

What does it mean on a practical level? It means that you're here to master your life and master the elements presented to you within the frequency, vibration, and theme presented by the Master number. *It means that you have some significant strengths and will experience some intense challenges.*

The bottom line: It's not easy!

The Master numbers are innately in conflict with themselves. Master numbers not only demand that you step up and take the lead in life, they also make conflicting demands on you. Let me explain.

Let's look at the Master number 11/2 as an example. The 11 is a double number 1—which means it's all about the self, creativity, initiation, independence, innovation, and self-confidence. Yet the foundational energy for the 11 is the number 2, which is all about others, partnership, group dynamics, being supportive, and behind the scenes. Can you see how—if you're on an 11/2 Life Path—you might feel conflicted most of the time? You must decide when to emphasize individuality and when to emphasize others, when to step forward yourself and when to stand behind someone else.

When you understand the demands the Master numbers exert, you can begin to work with yourself in more effective ways that can potentially harness all that amazingness you have to offer without causing you to crash and burn in the process. And this crash-and-burn phenomenon or consistent, intense frustration may be reoccurring themes you see in your life when engaged with the intensity of the Master numbers.

Just because you have a Master number doesn't mean you're superior. In actuality, you've enrolled in cosmic boot camp. For life. Yes. For. Life. Period. And remember, one of the critical components of any boot-camp experience is that it's meant to *level the ego, instill high levels of self-discipline*, and train you to *endure severe circumstances*. It's also training you to take the lead while also being the ultimate team player.

Working with Master numbers is a marathon, not a sprint. You must train, be flexible, pace yourself, and invest in the right equipment. Otherwise, you'll burn out quickly, or you'll deaden the flame of your passion and always feel as if you missed your chance for more yet will never find the courage or strength to take risks and move yourself and your enterprises to the next and higher level.

You're also being schooled to develop and act with *humility.* The Master numbers always bring heightened levels of ego to the game. Therefore, you'll be on the fast track to level and soften your ego without sublimating your superior gifts. You must connect with a sincere and deep sense of humility before you can manifest and harness the power of the Master numbers.

As his Holiness Pope Francis said in his 2017 TED Talk: "Please allow me to say it loudly and clearly. The more powerful you are, the more your actions will have an impact on people, the more responsible you are to act humbly. If you don't, your power will ruin you, and it will ruin the other."[1]

Another interesting observation to make about the Master numbers is this: Both the 11/2 and the 22/4 have the number 2 as a central theme. The core energy of the 2 is *love*—love, peace, patience, diplomacy, intuition, emotion, and relationship. So, keep this in the forefront of your mind as you consider some of the foundational challenges and goals that come with both the 11 and the 22. A common occurrence for people working with the Master number mission is that it can turn into feelings of being overwhelmed, resulting in not stepping up or into a higher-level calling.

Numerologist Matthew Goodwin suggests that it isn't possible to operate at the high level of the Master number all the time. He goes on to say that "Master number energy is there to be used if and when a person is ready. The Master number tension is present whether or not the power is used."[2]

If you have one or more Master numbers in your chart, more than likely you:
- Require additional sleep.
- Live with a consistently high level of anxiety.
- Grapple with a sense of intermittent depression.
- Have food sensitivities.
- Require more exercise.
- Feel as if you're never doing or being "enough."
- Know you were "meant for more."
- Need additional "down time," even if it's challenging for you to take it.
- Have experienced several profound "reinvention points" in your life.
- Have trouble "getting it together."
- Are extremely intuitive.
- Have an underlying drive to achieve great things in the world.
- Go through periods of time where you want to retreat from the world or "give up."
- Feel a burning urgency to find and pursue your purpose in life.
- Feel an obsession to accomplish something substantial.

What I want to stress is that once you learn the defining qualities of each of the numbers 1–9 in numerology, you can begin to learn how to apply that knowledge whenever the number shows up. It's a matter of understanding how to "plug in" the information effectively. Every number brings specific lessons with it. So, while the push inside us is toward manifesting the optimal aspects of our numbers, there is also a consistent pull from the oppositional elements our numbers encompass. When any number presents itself in a chart, we can be assured that it holds both the constructive/ and destructive elements—and sometimes overactive and underactive elements.

Keep in mind as you carry on with your study of numerology that the mission each number carries with it can appear to be challenging you with precisely the opposite of what you might expect. For instance, if you're learning about freedom, the chances are high that you'll grapple with restrictions of some kind. If you're learning how to be joyful and optimistic, chances are that you'll wrestle with hopelessness and pessimism. If you're learning about compassion, chances are you'll grapple with self-centeredness. Knowing the optimal manifestation of each number offers you information about the core issues each brings to the table.

NUMBERS 1–9 IN A GLANCE

NUMBER 1: The 1 is the leader and is learning about independence and confidence. It relates to new opportunity, inspiration, new starts, initiation, standing alone, originality, courage, concentration, determination, and leadership.

NUMBER 2: The 2 is a lover, not a fighter. It is learning about love, patience, and diplomacy. The 2 relates to love, emotional sensitivity, teamwork, cooperation, partnerships, details, serving group dynamics, harmony, and peace.

NUMBER 3: The 3 is the communicator and is learning about creative self-expression and emotional sensitivity. The 3 relates to joy, self-improvement, humor, artistic creativity, communication, performance, scattered focus, and dramatic emotional ups and downs.

NUMBER 4: The 4 is the systems builder and is learning about stability, security, and effective process. The 4 relates to material interests, structure, managing finances, creating lasting foundations, hard work, management, organization, efficiency, physical endurance, and limitations.

NUMBER 5: The 5 is the freedom seeker and is learning about fearlessness, adventure, and managing positive change. The 5 relates to sensuality, sales, sex, freedom, travel, communication, changes, flexibility, excitement, and adventure.

NUMBER 6: The 6 is the nurturer and is learning about responsibility, home, and family. The 6 relates to home, family, relationships, marriage, divorce, romance, responsibility, harmony, teaching, and justice.

NUMBER 7: The 7 is the spiritual seeker and is learning about trust, spirituality, and the depths of "self." It relates to mysticism, faith, intuition, inner growth, examination, study, analysis, reflection, mental acuity, specialization, philosophy, solitude, and refinement.

NUMBER 8: The 8 is the master of the material world and is learning about finances, empowerment, and authority. It relates to ethics, influence, money, business success (and failure), control, status, loss, gain, executive administration, management, ego, and personal power.

NUMBER 9: The 9 is the compassionate humanitarian and is learning about limited rewards, letting go, and philanthropy. It relates to unconditional love, humanitarianism, leadership by example, dramatic endings, emotional love, emotional crisis, the finer things in life, conclusions, compassion, magnetism, travel, idealism, charity, artistry, creativity, spirituality, romance, and forgiveness.

BIRTH CHARTS

CHAPTER 5

Here are just a few examples of "complex" birth charts. As you read these, you may be interested to hold in mind the notion that the archetype of a person with an 11/2 is the Channel, with a 22/4 is the Manifestor, and with a 33/6 is the Healer and Master Teacher. See if those archetypes seem to match what you know about the celebrities I have chosen. *Disclaimer:* Name and birthdate information is derived from biographical profiles published on Wikipedia.

BIRTH NAME:	Jerome Allen Seinfeld
CURRENT NAME:	Jerry Seinfeld
BIRTHDATE:	April 29, 1954

LIFE PATH:	16/7
EXPRESSION:	22/4
SOUL URGE:	14/5
BIRTHDAY:	11/2
PERSONALITY:	8
MATURITY:	11/2

BIRTH NAME:	Oprah Gail Winfrey
CURRENT NAME:	Oprah Winfrey
BIRTHDATE:	January 29, 1954

LIFE PATH:	13/4
EXPRESSION:	7
SOUL URGE:	11/2
BIRTHDAY:	11/2
PERSONALITY:	5
MATURITY:	11/2

BIRTH NAME:	Matthew David McConaughey
CURRENT NAME:	Matthew McConaughey
BIRTHDATE:	November 4, 1969

LIFE PATH:	22/4
EXPRESSION:	11/2
SOUL URGE:	11/2
BIRTHDAY:	4
PERSONALITY:	9
MATURITY:	6

BIRTH NAME:	Anthony J. Mahavoric
CURRENT NAME:	Tony Robbins
BIRTHDATE:	February 29, 1960

LIFE PATH:	11/2
EXPRESSION:	8
SOUL URGE:	13/4
BIRTHDAY:	11/2
PERSONALITY:	4
MATURITY:	1

BIRTH NAME:	Christine Michelle Metz
CURRENT NAME:	Chrissy Metz
BIRTH DATE:	September 29, 1980

LIFE PATH:	11/2
EXPRESSION:	11/2
SOUL URGE:	11/2
BIRTHDAY:	11/2
PERSONALITY:	9
MATURITY:	22/4

BIRTH NAME:	Peter Hayden Dinklage
CURRENT NAME:	Peter Dinklage
BIRTHDATE:	June 11, 1969

LIFE PATH:	33/6
EXPRESSION:	13/4
SOUL URGE:	11/2
BIRTHDAY:	11/2
PERSONALITY:	11/2
MATURITY:	1

There are other numbers in a full chart and indeed an entirely different realm of cycles. The most vital periods where Master numbers can show up in your chart are the Personal Year and Pinnacle cycles, which are critical components in your personality profile. They show up similarly—and yet differently overall—when they influence or guide a particular cycle in your life. Read about cycles in Part Five, "Exploring Cycles."

PART TWO

11/2

CHAPTER 6

MASTER NUMBER 11/2

"I told you so."
—Sincerely, your intuition

If you have the Master number 11/2 anywhere in your chart, then on top of the essential characteristics of the number 2 you possess added strengths and will confront intense challenges. To fully understand what this could signify for you, it's necessary to be aware of the attributes of the number 2, which provides the foundational energy for an 11/2 that shows up as your Life Path number or in another location in the chart. You also need to understand the 1 energy. The 11/2 combination indicates powerful forces at work whether it's one of the core numbers in your personality profile or appears in one of your cycles.

Think of it this way: The 11/2 is like a sandwich cookie. The 2 is the "filling" and the 1s in the 11 hold the filling together on both sides!

First, we'll go over the number 1 and its meaning. Then we'll work with the number 2. We'll also build our understanding of how these numbers engage and interact with each other—looking for how they may enhance each other and how they may clash.

The Master number 11/2 is the most recognized Master number in numerology, so we'll dig a bit deeper here to set the stage for this enigmatic number. When it shows up in your chart, it indicates that your special mission—a task that goes above and beyond the scope of the task outlined by the number 2—is to recognize and use your creativity, intuition, and healing abilities for the benefit of humanity. You can achieve this in a multitude of ways, such as by eliciting an emotional response through dance, music, film, or art. Or by working one-on-one with people or in groups using various healing modalities. You can write, entertain, or teach—or do any other activity, service, or interaction that engages you in endeavors where you touch the lives of people on a grand yet sometimes intangible or immeasurable scale. In her book *Master Numbers,* Faith Javane asserts that "the vibrations of number 11 are dynamic and extreme, and must be used with great wisdom. Number Elevens will naturally fall into leadership positions, and this requires the best humanitarian qualities they can muster. They will realize eventually that true mastership is service to others."[1]

Remember, this number holds a double 1—which is all about leadership and confidence—and yet also a 2—which is all about harmony and love. It also comes with unique challenges for those who would fulfill its mission. The 11 is more of an etheric experience for both you and those around you. And what I mean is this: You offer healing energies just by your sheer presence—you honestly don't have to *do* anything. Do people ever tell you that they feel better after talking with you? That they feel calmer just sitting in the same room with you?

Or you might be that 11/2 who draws people to your flame, yet you present more with the energy of the 1 than of the 2. In this case, you may come across as loving—with an edge. Think about 11/2 Life Path's Jennifer Aniston, Tony Robbins, or Stephen Colbert. Indeed, these folks present with the assertion of the number 1 and yet we can also feel some of their "soft center."

Many numerologists say that as an 11/2 you're a dreamer rather than a doer. You must work at getting your head out of the clouds and coming down and operating on *terra firma.* Understand that you're here to share your gifts through creative work—healing, art, performance, music, diplomacy, or as an inventor. Your contributions can often elude you because your creations change people's lives, yet sometimes not in a measurable way. It's like when a person goes to an exhibit and takes in the piece of art, and by engaging in that experience, the viewer is altered in some way. It's not tangible. People can't put their finger on it. They'll go away from experiencing your work of art changed or have an internal shift in some immeasurable way. Metaphorically, and sometimes literally, that's the energy of the 11/2.

Twos will go out of their way to avoid being in the spotlight. A 2 is most at peace and satisfied when running the show from behind the curtain, and just the thought of getting out in front of people can make the 2 extremely nervous. The Master number 11/2 pushes you into the spotlight, and this will have disconcerting effects. You're extremely sensitive to criticism and putting yourself out there will always bring criticism from outside forces—and that always places you outside of your comfort zone. You, of all people, need to learn the fine and consistent art of psychic self-protection and become an expert in not taking things personally. You'll have a nervous energy that you just can't control. You'll lean toward impatience and criticism—both toward yourself and others—and you're going to arm-wrestle with self-confidence. You can also grapple with undisciplined emotions in a way that drives a wedge between you and your higher calling.

The Master number 11/2 sets you up for doing battle with a reasonably hefty ego, which is ironic because you actually volley from feeling entirely inferior to loftily superior—back and forth. This number sets you up for inspired leadership and achievement, yet you'll most likely feel as if you're perpetually jumping through rings of fire to get there.

Numerologist Matthew Goodwin maintains that the Master 11/2 "must work to develop intuition . . . and must stand ready to be a channel with a message from above."[1] The 11/2 must "inspire by his own example, living in the way revealed to him, spreading his illumination for others to absorb and benefit. This number is as difficult as it is rewarding."[2]

If you're astrologically inclined, you might deepen your connection with the number 11 by its association with the Chiron figure. You might even think of yourself as a "Wounded Healer" because your life provides you with plenty of obstacles to get your footing, to embrace your high level of spirituality and intuition, and then act upon your gifts in a way that will infuse and ignite your presence into the world. In her book *Numerology*, Juno Jordan notes that the Master 11/2 has the "inner power to influence the masses and bring Light to humanity."[3] She also asserts that there is a tendency for the 11/2 to get swept away with its power and ability to lead.

If spiritual living isn't present with the Master 11/2, the person will often suffer a downfall. As Faith Javane asserts: "If these individuals use their Master numbers to glorify themselves, however, they will experience loss and unhappiness. The Eleven is a very severe vibration to handle."[4]

Matthew Goodwin suggests that the overall challenge for the 11/2 is that when it is being negatively expressed it denies the energy of the 2. Instead of being sensitive, cooperative, and considerate, the propensity is to be too sensitive, which shows up as being extremely shy, uncertain, and sometimes apathetic or indifferent.[5]

I know several 11/2 Life Paths who have an online presence through blogging and other services and it's fascinating to see how many times they use the word *love* in their communications. "I love this; I love that, I love, love, love." These are the folks who use hearts to dot their Is and heart icons to punctuate every sentence. They are overflowing with love and frame their communication in this way. Framing communication in this way is often a central characteristic of the energy of the number 2. When it comes to the 11, the double 1s bring an edge or a more forceful feeling to this core loving energy. It feels like a harder form of love that's centered more on the self than the love of the 2, which is softer and more focused on the other.

Hans Decoz remarks that the 11/2 often is misunderstood by others early in life and this can result in the 11/2 becoming very shy, timid, and withdrawn. Misreading the 11/2 is usually how an 11/2 starts out in life—as being so overly sensitive that no one (especially the young 11/2) realizes to what extent the 11/2 is being clobbered with emotional shrapnel every single day.

Decoz also makes the point that as an 11/2 "you galvanize every situation you enter. You inspire people, but without your conscious effort. Energy seems to flow through you without your control. The energy that permeates through you gives both power, and sometimes, emotional turmoil."[6]

A key element to grasp is that the number 11/2 has great connectivity to outer realms where thoughts, energy, and ideas reside. Decoz asserts: "Ideas, thoughts, understanding, and insight can come to you without your having to go through a rational thought process."[7] The 11/2 has an excellent capacity for invention and the formulation of ideas. Often inventors, artists, political figures, prophets, and spiritual leaders have an 11 prominent in their chart.

As an 11/2, you're not only emotionally sensitive, you're over-the-top intuitive. The 11/2 energy matrix requires that you build and use your emotional psychic shield daily or you'll become so emotionally paralyzed you won't have the strength or endurance to fulfill your mission. You're highly intuitive and have healing energy, whether you're directly working in the healing circuit or offering your power to others through whatever other form of work you choose. You're at your best when you're helping others to heal and transform through your selfless service and artistic creativity. Be mindful that artistic creativity can take many forms—everything from dance, to healing, writing, performing, creative problem solving, and beyond. Also understand that you're not meant to be a "hand-holder." The 2 is more of a "hands-on" personality, while the Master 11/2 takes the lead while offering instruction or setting an example for others.

Overall, you're complicated and layered. There's so much more going on under the surface with you than anyone can ever guess or understand. As you develop and mature, your intuition will form a vibrant and fertile foundation for all your efforts. Your emotional acuity can be an asset rather than a destructive force once it's trained and developed. Since you're a dreamer, you're full of inspired ideas and creative impulses. There is both a heady and airy quality to you. You can want big things and yet sometimes lack the courage or confidence to make it into a reality. You can often be extremely misread because you're a walking contradiction—or at least what one might call a *real handful.*

Hans Decoz makes the point that the 11/2 possesses excellent abilities and yet indulges in an overabundance of self-reflection and self-criticism. He also observes—rightly so—that the 11/2 undergoes a vast amount of inner development. Hans states that if you are an 11/2 this internal development "takes precedence over your ability to materialize the great undertaking you were chosen to perform—and therefore the 11/2 often develops more slowly and it takes a long time to develop the confidence to step into your higher calling."[8]

Stephen Colbert has an 11/2 Life Path. He's a practicing Catholic, family centered, and a successful actor and comedian. In an interview with Oprah Winfrey on *Super Soul Sunday* at the Apollo Theatre in 2018, he speaks of God's edict that he calls the "harrowing journey" of loving your neighbor as you love yourself. He goes on to observe that the most difficult element is to love the people you don't agree with—citing that it's easy to love the people you *do* agree with! He says: "What gives me hope is that *love* is not a bad word. That we can say 'love' or 'I love,' or 'love is the only/every God,' . . . to say love is the most important thing and to say it without embarrassment."[9]

Colbert talks about Spike Jones interviewing him prior to the launch of *The Late Show with Stephen Colbert*, which was ostensibly a real risk for him after leaving his extremely highly rated *The Colbert Report* on Comedy Central. He said that several months after the show launched, Jones sent him the notes from the interview to remind him what his intention was when he was developing the program. Colbert said that his intention went like this: "I don't know how to do a nightly comedy show that's also about love. But I'd like it in some way to be about love. And there's so many ways to express that, I suppose."[10]

I personally find it fun and useful to listen to the words people use and see how it aligns with themes represented in their numerology profile. For instance, obviously a primary focus for Master 11/2 Life Path Stephen Colbert is the word *love*. The essence of the number 2, as you know, is love. Often people who carry the Master 11/2 in their charts express themselves this way. "I love this," "I love that." Notice how many people would never emote that way or communicate that way and yet for an 11/2, life is centered on love and forms the foundation from which all things radiate.

Stephen Colbert offers yet another example of the intriguing dichotomy of the Master 11/2. Even as he speaks of God and love as integral parts of his life and work, Colbert is not shy about the pleasure he derives in being the number one-rated late-night talk show. During his interview, Oprah asked him if it felt the same to be number one as it does to be number two, to which he replies: "Nope. It feels a little better!"[11]

Of all the Master numbers, the 11/2 contains the most oppositional qualities. The 2 and the 4 of the 22/4 are more simpatico—they "get" each other. The same goes for the 3 and the 6 of the 33/6. The 1 and the 2 couldn't be more different from each other, and so it takes added effort and mindfulness to provide them with the best environment so that they may grow together.

CHAPTER 7

NUMBER 1

1

AT ITS BEST

A 1's optimal expression is boldness, innovation, risk-taking, resilience, and following the inner voice. Its mission is to develop creativity and confidence. Its purpose is to bring positive, creative energy into the world and to achieve independence even as it relates with others. A born leader and innovator, the 1 is self-motivated, independent, and hard working. It thrives in a competitive environment, although ironically it is hypersensitive to criticism.

STEPS ON THE LADDER

The 1 engages in three specific stages of development: dependency, rebellion, and actualization. It's meant to learn healthy independence and therefore often finds itself—particularly early on—in situations where it's very much *dependent*. A sense of dependence can be anything that feels that the 1 is being asked to fit in and be defined by external forces. Despite this, down deep the 1 knows that the way it is being asked to behave or look isn't representative of its uniqueness or individuality. It can take a while for the 1 to understand and define what it is that's blocking its sense of independence.

The second stage of development is *rebellion.* Once the 1 decides that it wants to break free of any dependence, it revolts. Often it takes a while for the 1 to learn a healthy and empowering way of differentiation. The rebellious stage usually expresses as some form of self-destruction. Or alternately, there may be a period when the 1 wants to rebel and can't find the courage—and then patterns of frustration and anger can begin to define the held-back number 1.

The third tier of development shows up after the 1 has done its work, as they say. The stage of *actualization* comes when the 1 identifies where it feels dependent and has extracted itself from that dependence in a way that is both realistic and healthy. When the 1 finishes with the rebellious phase it is ready to get to work establishing itself in the world of creation, innovation, and leadership.

STANDING STRONG

As an individualist, the 1 is unique in every way. When it's insecure, it feels like Mork from *Mork and Mindy*—like it's a being from another planet that's just trying to fit in somehow. The 1 feels misplaced, as if it doesn't fit in or belong anywhere. When the 1 is authentic, it's kind, trustworthy, compassionate, and compelling. When it isn't confident, it tends to be pushy, defensive, aggressive, and angry. Those outlets manifest when the 1 suffers from lack of self-esteem. Reaching a level of expertise instills the 1 with a solid sense of self-confidence. With a 1, having complete trust in skills learned and mastered serves as a kind of "security blanket" when feeling insecure or when self-esteem is under fire. Having the ability to fall back on high-level skills stabilizes the 1. The 1 must understand that it's not meant to follow the crowd—on the contrary. It's the one who's the odd duck. The sooner the 1 learns to *"embrace its weird"* the better off it'll be.

The 1 will never fit into the mold. Its gift is to believe in ideas, galvanize plans, and take strategic and calculated risks. The fail rate will be higher than most, yet that's because the 1 tries more and takes more risks on a much more consistent basis than most try in an entire lifetime.

NEW IDEAS, ANYONE?

The 1 is a pioneer and innovator who is capable of great success and achievement. In fact, it's the birthright of the number 1 to be an achiever. It needs to be in charge and managing in some way. It makes a great entrepreneur or inventor. Often the highest and best use of the number 1 is when it masterminds a project, gets it up and running, makes sure management systems are in place, and then is off to the next venture. The 1 might feel stagnant, bored, or underutilized if it isn't allowed to tackle new challenges. It's full of creative energy, and this innovative force is the gift of the 1. The 1 thrives when it imagines new things, introduces new concepts, and then delegates the details, and either moves on with another project or continues developing a plan while taking it to the next level of success.

The 1 enjoys being on the move and having a variety of things to do. The keys to this are confidence, preparation, and focus. The number 1 can choose to be the absentminded professor or low-level administrative assistant—or it can take itself seriously enough to train well, get a proper education, and expand its horizons. The 1's purpose is to create things, whether those are new ideas or new products and services. It strives to be "number one" and can use its innate competitive spirit to move ideas forward into reality.

RISKY BUSINESS

Anything that calls for tapping into a unique voice, independent action, and decision-making is the forte of the number 1. The 1 begs development of a sense of risk and learns to embrace a level of uncertainty. As the 1 develops leadership skills, it's required to nurture the best in others and understand that creativity flourishes in an atmosphere of inner security and confidence—meaning it must open up and step off the beaten path. Its constant challenge is to consistently and consciously develop a sense of self-assurance, inner direction, and centeredness while also considering the needs of others.

When the 1 expresses itself from the heart and not just the head, it can achieve great things. But the 1 must be careful of succumbing to feelings of superiority, judgment, or criticism. It's most useful when working directly with people and keying into their innate gifts and strengths. It can achieve its highest potential from accepting or developing leadership roles. The 1 thrives in an environment where there are ample rewards for innovation and achievement and when it is the center of attention, looked up to, and admired.

IS IT ALWAYS THIS DIFFICULT?

The 1 rivals the number 8 in the "school of hard knocks." If the 1 is meant to be a pioneer, inventor, entrepreneur—or whatever other aspects of life it taps into and uses to express its creative and revolutionary ideas—then certainly the 1 will undergo many false starts. It's not meant to play it safe or color within the lines. As a result, the 1 benefits from understanding that it won't necessarily acquire rousing acceptance or constant approval. Even though on some level the 1 knows this, it also has an internal soft spot for acknowledgment and approval. It craves "rah-rahs."

There's been a lot written about "failing forward." This concept could be the mantra for the number 1. The mission of the 1 isn't the easy route. Its path isn't linear or safe. The 1 cultivates the power of persistence. It falls and gets back up again, taking the lessons gleaned from the fall into the next experience to derive successful results.

GROUND CONTROL TO MAJOR TOM

The number 1 needs to be in charge. It's the leader, so it needs followers. It's not the best at sharing power and control. It can often mistake the creation of a healthy love relationship when it feels it's giving someone a share of power. Romantic relationships are defined by the 1 and controlled by the 1. Often the 1 attracts partners who are more like students. When the student absorbs all the 1 has to give, then the relationship disintegrates. While the 1 has a commanding presence, often it chooses partners who are unequal—this can be in business as well as personal engagements.

Only when the 1 attracts and picks someone who is its equal intellectually, financially, and spiritually will it be able to maintain and thrive in a relationship. And that takes learning to maintain self-confidence while keeping its ego at bay and learning to modulate power in the connection and understand the needs of the other. The 1 needs a cheerleader, yet cheerleading can turn to empty accolades when expressions of admiration travel a one-way street. Since the i is learning about independence and individuality, it struggles to overcome a strong sense of self-centeredness, making it hard to understand the true nature of a balanced relationship. The i benefits when coming to the table ready, willing, and able to co-create, and forgoing the need for absolute control in exchange for the balance of mutual respect and a balance of authority within the relationship.

THE FLIPSIDE OF NUMBER 1

CHAPTER 8

THE DEVIL ON YOUR SHOULDER

One of the major obstacles to maintaining the optimal version of the number 1 is its broad sense of self-doubt and crippling lack of self-esteem. The 1 is often sidetracked by a nonstop voice of criticism in its head, whispering incessantly: *You're not good enough. Who do you think you are? Nobody's ever done that before.* That voice is a decoy that leads the 1 away from its true power. Since the life of the 1 is rife with lessons involving failure, it's easy for the 1 to become beaten down. The 1 is primed to color outside of the lines, think outside of the box, and make things happen that don't fit the existing structure or follow the existing rules. It isn't meant to fit in and the more it embraces and acts upon its uniqueness, the better off and more successful it is.

WERE WE TALKING ABOUT ME?

The number 1 is the number of self—of *the self*. The 1 is all about being "number one." And so, it's no wonder that one of the flipsides for the 1 is self-centeredness and ego identification—sometimes to the point of narcissism. The 1 is learning a healthy sense of self, and that makes all issues relating to dependence and independence, as well as individuality and achievement, focal points. It's meant to lead and exert itself and at the same time also to learn how to consider others and work with others practically. The 1 often institutes a "my way or the highway" attitude, particularly after creating a certain amount of success. The 1 is always learning how to be an efficient and robust leader—not a dictator.

NOT RISING TO THE CHALLENGE

A downside to the energy of the 1 comes into play when it isn't rising to the challenge: when it finds itself dependent, lacking creative outlet, or responding to an unrelenting internal sense of inadequateness. Then it can default to presenting a wall of judgment to the world. The underlying reason for to the 1 to dole out such harsh punishment to those around it is so that the 1 doesn't feel responsible for where it finds itself if it isn't actively achieving or being independent. It's a deflection mechanism. The 1 can be a bully who concentrates all its energy on berating others so that it doesn't become the target of harassment or criticism. It acts like it's the one who has been wronged. Being a victim of other people's incompetence, for instance, can feel more palatable to the 1 than itself failing to initiate change. The 1 can opt to find the negatives in virtually everything instead of itself. As it judges those around it, it's easy to see fault everywhere. Finding the bad and the ugly is easy. It's much more challenging to be a problem solver and visionary, which is the birthright of the number 1.

DEFLECTIVE TACTICS

The 1 can exchange robust leadership for petty bullying. It rivals the 4 in assertiveness and the need to be right. There's a delicate balance with the initiating and achieving energy of the 1, as acts related to these can easily topple over into applications of blunt force. The 1 is interested in a winning outcome, but not necessarily a win/win outcome. Its focus is most often on negotiating a competitive advantage and a winning result for itself, which may come at the expense of someone or something else. It's the rule of the jungle, after all—and the 1 is heavy on negotiation and light on mediation. It can be challenging for the 1 even to care about someone else's point of view. The eye is on the prize and the 1 generally knows what it takes to get there. Typically, the 1 projects strength. And if there is a weak underbelly, the 1 makes darn sure that it's entirely camouflaged and protected. Remember, the real reason for resorting to judgment and pushiness is to detract from personal weaknesses. Given that the 1 is learning how to wield power and take the lead—and often grapples with a strange lack of self-confidence—it makes sense that it might deflect some of the broader issues at hand with some assertive bullying.

I have noticed a common denominator with several people who have 1 Life Paths who have consistently struggled with the flipside of the calling and lessons of the number 1. I'll give a composite of several men who have very similar issues they've grappled with throughout their lives. They all were leaders in their field and enjoyed high levels of prestige and a certain level of power. All were highly intelligent and had a rather scathing sense of humor that dipped heavily into sarcasm and "dark" humor. Alcohol became their addiction of choice and alcoholism fueled their inability to connect with others and was particularly damaging to their family lives; showing up as marriages, divorces, long-standing feuds with friends, and traumatized off-spring. All of these men have passed on, yet even at the end of life, they couldn't see the effects and the collateral damage related to their self-centeredness and narcissism. I don't want to be Debbie-Downer, yet we all know and deal with people who live out the extremes of the flipside of their mission in life.

CHAPTER 9

NUMBER2

AT ITS BEST

The number 2 seeks harmony and profoundly loathes conflict. It works hard to avoid conflict and confrontation and yet often finds itself amid unrest. It's the peacekeeper. It's an understatement to observe that the blessing of the 2 is also its curse. To engage in mediation, what's needed? That's right: *conflict.* And there's not a lot that gives the 2 an upset stomach more than conflict. The 2's calling is to be a diplomatic presence; therefore, it attracts certain levels of battle on a consistent basis. Rather than curse this phenomenon or waste time wondering why it continuously draws people or experiences into play that require heightened levels of diplomacy and mediation, do your best to recognize and accept that the powerful lessons the 2 energy offers you cannot be derived from the avoidance of conflict. Conflict is a requirement for the 2's personal growth.

This is part of the purpose of the 2: to create win-win outcomes in the face of adversity. The 2 isn't the Negotiator archetype; it's the *Mediator.* It doesn't thrive on one person or entity coming out on top as the *winner* while another is the *loser.* It always seeks fairness, peace, and serenity. Optimally, the 2 develops firm, yet supple boundaries and enough emotional resiliency to serve as a master mediator.

ALL YOU NEED IS LOVE

The 2 energy is all about *love* and *relationship.* It's here to love others and re-ceive love in return. The 2's theme song? Cheap Trick's "I Want You to Want Me." It craves the giving and receiving of unconditional love yet may have no clue what the term *unconditional* means. And since the number 2 is the number of love and relationship, the 2 is *learning about* relationships. That means it requires a lot of practice! That desire combined with a strong sense of service and emotional sensitivity brings about beautiful things, as well as consistent challenges. The trick is not to focus on needing love to the point of desperation.

The true mission of the 2 involves setting healthy emotional boundaries and getting to know itself deeply and profoundly. Only then will it attract the partnerships that offer the unconditional love, admiration, and support that it craves. Since the 2 is so sensitive and wants to exchange love all the time, it tends to smother its loved ones or have unrealistic expectations of them. The number 2 contains a powerful combination of strength and sensitivity that doesn't always show on the surface.

The 2 tends to gravitate toward family life and desires to serve as a supportive, dependable, caring helpmate when working with its most favorable aspects.

SHIVERING WITH ANTICI . . . PATION

Two is the number of patience. Anytime a 2 shows up in your chart, it means there will be delays, frustrations, and a need for trust in the process and the patience that goes with it. Also, understand that when a 2 is prevalent, *timing* is crucial. Keep in mind that often the reason for delays and frustrations is right timing is unfolding at its own pace. So, do your best to go with the flow, use your intuition, and stay open to guidance—as opposed to *pushing* for results and *making* things happen. There are times when attempting to pound a round peg into a square hole won't work. The 2 is feminine energy. It is heart-centered, fluid, and nurturing.

WEARING YOUR HEART ON YOUR SLEEVE

The energy of the 2 is *exceptionally emotionally sensitive*, so when it shows up there is heightened opportunity for hurt feelings in ways few can understand. The 2 doesn't understand the degree to which it's emotionally wounded day in and day out. It wears its heart on its sleeve, and this often becomes detrimental because of the emotional battering it experiences.

To say it's an emotional sponge is an understatement. The gift of the 2 is that it has psychic levels of emotional radar and can walk into a room and scan everyone's emotional barometer. While that's all well and good, a problem arises when the 2 can't filter out everyone else's energy from its own. The 2 often *takes on* the emotions of others, to the point of being drained and confounded about why it feels drained, unacknowledged, used, and abused. People often use the 2 as a trash can for their psychic garbage. The 2 must learn not to be a doormat.

INTUITIVE LIGHTNING ROD

The 2 is highly intuitive, which is an offshoot or direct result of its high emotional sensitivity. When the 2 is in flow, it is grace, patience, love, and caring in motion. The 2 can intuit everyone's emotional states and with practice, because the 2 is so highly attuned, the 2 can learn to use this gift in myriad ways, including, but not limited to, healing itself and others. It often takes the 2 a specified period to learn its own intuitive language. The 2 in some ways knows it has extrasensory perception and yet will often talk itself out of acknowledging and embracing that aspect of itself.

ARTSY

Innately artistic, the 2 often excels in design or other creative endeavors that require a sense of refinement, balance, and coordination. The 2 seeks peace and creates peaceful surroundings. This trait can be expressed within a home or can extend into a career where the 2 establishes harmony through any kind of design skill that capitalizes on this innate talent: costume design, set design, interior design, interior staging, photography, or cake decoration to name a few possibilities. While the 2 is creative, its creativity thrives when it can operate in the background or a supportive position. When you find the 2 in entertainment, in the form of the actor, musician, or any other performance artist, the chances are high that there is an 11/2 in the mix. Most 2s don't naturally gravitate toward the limelight.

IT'S ALL ABOUT EVERYONE ELSE

The 2 is happiest when it is being of service to family or its group or community of choice. Detail oriented, it's the one everyone turns to get the job done and get it done right. As it thrives in an environment of support and solid direction, when a 2 is present the energy is conducive to working within a group dynamic or in one-on-one partnership. The 2 may struggle to find success working solo or as an independent contractor. Envision the 2 as Oprah Winfrey's devoted assistant, not Oprah! The 2 is the power behind the throne and would rather die than be thrust into the lead or the spotlight. Leave that for other more communicative numbers. The 2 feels warm and fuzzy when it's in the know, making things happen, ensuring everything runs smoothly, and when the outcome is pleasant and positive for all involved.

I have a friend (let's call her Daphne) who personifies the major elements of the number 2. She's always sunny, cheerful, and high energy. Daphne's life revolves around her family, both her husband of 20 years, his family, and her family of origin. She's worked in various helping professions and yet her primary focus is on her extended support and engagement with her family. This comes into play in all kinds of ways: traveling to stay with her aunt whose husband is being moved to a nursing home, supporting her husband as he goes through a lawsuit, or always being there for her friends and offering both small and larger gestures of love on a consistent basis. She finds profound satisfaction in living her life with this level of giving and providing support for those she cares about. She also takes great care of herself and makes sure she treats herself as well as she treats others. Daphne decided early on that she didn't want children and yet she nurtures everyone around her, from her dogs to her husband to her friends. She happens to have a 2 Life Path and seems to relish and act upon the more positive expression of the loving and diplomatic number 2.

THE FLIPSIDE OF NUMBER 2

CHAPTER 10

THE COMBAT ZONE

Sometimes the number 2 takes the opposite route from togetherness and harmony, and its default is a combative posture. When combative and agitated, it responds to situations in a reactive way rather than in an empathetic or give-and-take manner. The agitation of the 2 stems from a broad sense of feeling walked on and wounded. Its defense is either striking first before being struck or putting up a fortress of protection that manifests as being blunt, aggressive, and employing self-centered forms of engagement. Ultimately the 2 must come to terms with its hypersensitivity and come to an accurate conclusion that other people don't necessarily see the world and take it in with the same profound emotional acuity as it does.

The task of the 2 is to construct psychic armor to protect itself from the onslaught of emotional energy that it tends to take personally. Only with protection and healthy detachment can the 2 find its own identity and—by extension—healthy modes of expression. The 2 would benefit from reading the chapter in *The Four Agreements* by don Miguel Ruiz on not taking things personally. If this is you, keep that book in an easy-to-access place on your desk or nightstand.

The 2 implodes when it feels that everyone is asking too much from it. It can have a lot of the "straw that broke the camel's back" moments where it can meltdown during a seemingly innocent interaction because internally it feels as if it's reached the last straw.

DOWN THE DRAIN

The trademark of the 2 is a tendency to do everything for everybody around it to the point where it feels drained, unappreciated, and unacknowledged. Even though the 2 is wired to serve and love, it often gives itself a little too much credit. The irony is that a priority of the 2 is to gain approval from outside sources continually. The 2 is always the one asking others what they think it should do, how it should make a decision, and if its butt looks big in these jeans. The primary "Ah-ha" for the 2 is to understand it isn't meant to receive emotional validation from external sources. Why not? Because learning to give itself its kudos is part of the overall lesson for the 2. The big reveal happens when the 2 learns how to receive the validation, love, and approval it needs from *itself*. Then and only then do the floodgates open and the acknowledgment and validation it's been virtually prostituting itself for magically starts rolling in—just in time for the 2 not to care about that anymore! As Byron Katie says: "Spare yourself from seeking love, approval, or appreciation from anyone. And watch what happens in reality."[1]

One of the interesting things to think about is that the 2 is very outer focused. It is concerned with what others think of it and how its performance and behavior are being judged. The tricky part is that—even though the 2 appears to be all about everyone else—in fact the 2 is just as self-focused as the number 1 (or any other number for that matter). The huge difference is that the 2 cares about others, is attuned to others, and creates its sense of worth by gauging its "approval rating" with others. This entirely derives from its unending and constant need for love, acceptance, and approval.

CODEPENDENT NO MORE

The number 2 makes a wonderfully codependent bedfellow (along with the number 3) in the undisciplined emotions department. Like an emotional lightning rod, the 2 is susceptible to emotional entanglement. It can take it a rather extensive amount of time to understand how ridiculously emotionally sensitive it is and begin to manage itself accordingly. Total immersion in others' feelings is its natural state of being. It takes a considerable amount of effort for the 2 to step back. But until it does, it won't recognize that most people don't experience life in the same intense manner.

This is the pivotal blessing and curse for the 2. The 2 is learning the power of balancing, harmonizing, and disciplining its emotional flow. The 2 is the consummate worrier and meddler, and anxiety should probably be its middle name. Left unchecked, the emotions of the 2 are a quagmire. The key for the 2 is to develop emotional maturity—and this takes a lot of practice! Trial and error, anyone? It's all about using emotional engagement *and* healthy detachment—and the 2's amazing intuition and emotional intelligence—for successful outcomes.

ME, MYSELF, AND TRYING TO BE WHOM I THINK EVERYONE ELSE THINKS I SHOULD BE

With the number 2, there is a loss of identity—or not so much a loss as a void of *healthy ego development*. Codependency is its natural habitat. It mutates itself to meet the needs—or the perceived needs—of those around it. Often the 2 judges itself and creates its sense of self and self-worth by *what it observes* everyone else saying about it. Simultaneously, it is making up its own story about what everyone else wants and needs and assuming this is reality. The challenge for the 2 is to develop an internal compass and turn inward for validation. It must be careful not to take on the problems of others, who are more than happy to allow it to do so.

Others—whether consciously or not—see the 2 as a psychic garbage pail and are more than happy to dump all their dirty energy there. It's best for the 2 not to place itself entirely at the disposal of others—despite its propensity and willingness to do so—because soon it comes back around to anger and resentment for being used and underappreciated. When living in the negative aspects of the 2 energy no one knows who it is or what it wants, including itself. It's too preoccupied doing whatever it thinks it's *supposed* to do and is quick to expect others do the same. It's in a chronic state of codependence and enmeshment. Giving turns to resentment, as it gives too much and then withdraws completely—all the while fuming with anger and frustration and wondering why no one appreciates everything it does.

Why can't anyone love me enough? is the frantic default thought for the 2. Only when the 2 realizes its entirely free to form its own lifestyle and follow its own internal guidance can it detach from the opinions of others and reach its potential. Until then, it guides itself from a skewed sense of what others expect from it.

STORMY WEATHER

The 2 may back away from pursuing love or allowing itself to be vulnerable enough to invite love in because it hurts too badly. When the 2 can come to an understanding of how to balance an intense need for love, it'll feel secure and supported. The trick is to give itself the acknowledgment it needs rather than seeking it from outside sources. A number 2 Life Path friend of mine in a fit of despair once said: "I guess I'm just meant to die alone!" which occurred after an emotionally unavailable boyfriend dumped her. Rather than reviewing her part in the relationship and taking charge of it, she fell into a childish victim mode and a deep depression, whereupon she refused to assist herself.

The 2's sense of hopelessness can be an unfortunate tendency. Sometimes the 2 feels as though it's the main character in the Johnny Lee song "Lookin' for Love (in All the Wrong Places)."

Its energy often leads the 2 to settle for getting love in a relationship that isn't altogether healthy. The reason for this is that the 2 is learning how to grow into and embrace itself, and this takes experience. It requires a strong desire to get to know itself on a genuine and authentic level. The 2 can feel unworthy of receiving the love it desires.

THE BLOB

In relationships, the 2 can be a shape shifter when challenged to exert its sense of self. It can lose its identity in partnership. The tendency of the 2 is in some ways to disappear into the perceived needs of the other. It tends to mutate into whatever it's placed next to. Like a chameleon, its goal is to change itself to blend into the environment. But this creates confusion, as the 2 often will attempt simultaneously and rather childishly, to keep the focus on itself—and will volley back and forth.

An example of this would be a 2 who feels she does everything for everyone in her family selflessly (her husband, kids, and extended family) and yet her marriage is unraveling because everything she does is done without consulting or communicating her decisions or actions with her husband. She will be flummoxed when her husband leaves her on the grounds of her emotional unavailability, lack of communication, and overinvolvement with her family of origin.

Only when the 2 steps into its own identity on a consistent basis is it able to attract more satisfying and positive outcomes in every area of its life.

I have known many people with 2s in their charts. If I were to offer an illustration of how the flipside of the number 2 can manifest, here is a composite of how it has played out. Let's call our flipside role model Courtney. Courtney loves to be loved. She loves to be needed. She got married and had children, only to find that her husband was an alcoholic. She divorced him and yet stayed ensconced in anger, judgment, and resentment about him, making it hard on her children to forge a relationship with their father. She has a mother who is both loving and tyrannical, who was not surprisingly also an alcoholic. On the one hand, she enabled Courtney by giving her money and on the other hand, she consistently criticized her for not being who she thought she should be.

In her forties, Courtney decided to pursue a career as a flight attendant, something she'd always dreamed of when she was younger. Her children were now grown up and she took the plunge, trained, and got a job with an airline. Yet her mother would demean her every time there was a family gathering, telling her that she'd never make any money doing that job and even more repugnant to her, she wasn't being a proper wife to her husband since her job took her out of town on a regular basis. Not surprisingly, Courtney got injured on the job, and then she quit.

Courtney's demeanor, far from being "soft and fuzzy," was abrasive and combative. In order to assert any sense of power, she was always the one returning her meal at a restaurant or telling off the cashier for doing something she considered to be wrong. She always made herself available to do things for the family and then would become outraged when her efforts weren't showered with accolades and appreciation.

When Courtney's husband left her for another woman she began questioning what her role has been in her relationships. Even though she has a long way to go, she's at least seeing that she can potentially begin to make different choices in her life that would result in clearer emotional boundaries and in getting to know herself on an entirely different and empowering level.

CHAPTER 11

BRINGING THE DOUBLE 1 INTO THE 2

The Master number 11/2 brings the double number 1 into partnership with the number 2. It's almost like it is a Siamese twin with two entirely different brains attached to one shared body. That it is conjoined is its magic, beauty, and harrowing journey. You may find it useful to conceptualize the Master 11/2 as two parts 1 with one part 2.

Here are five suggestions for introducing the energy of 1 to the energy of 2 so that they will be fluid and powerful dance partners.

LEAN ON ME

The Master 11/2 can present like a crusty geode, yet when you crack it open, it has a soft and gooey, sweet center. The double 1 offers plenty of power, assertiveness, and leadership—so much so that often it overpowers the gentler 2 in the process. When you understand the fact that you have a high-level masculine/feminine mix here, you can learn from both aspects of your personality. The emotionally sensitive 2 can reach out and draw upon the assertive 1 energy when lacking a sense of stability. And the self-oriented double 1 can reach into its bag of emotional connectivity that the 2 hides for safekeeping.

Often, choosing to tap into 1 energy or 2 energy depends on what's necessary in the moment. Having a choice is a gift. But it takes knowledge, finesse, and practice to choose well. Remember that the 1 is the negotiator while the 2 is the mediator. The 1 is all about me while the 2 is all about us. The 1 wants the spotlight while the 2 prefers to disappear at the sidelines—even if it would love to take all the credit for success. There can be a volley of these two styles of interacting and often the given circumstances of a situation will predicate which one.

Getting a divorce? Most likely the assertive 1 will show up for divorce court.

The first day of school for your son? Most likely the thoughtful and emotional 2 will show up with a homemade lunch and a hand-written note.

The number 2 is known to be self-sacrificing while the number 1 is known to be self-oriented. The 1 is initiating while the 2 is receptive. The 1 needs others to explain itself while the 2 feels the need to explain itself to others.

"HOW AM I DOING?"

While the double 1 brings in energy that's innovative and independent, it has something in common with the more relationship-oriented 2—the need for approval. It's beneficial for the 11/2 to understand that there can be a needy quality to it that's more digestible when this neediness is recognized and modulated. While the 11 is the dominant force in the 11/2 mix, insecurity may lay just beneath the bravado. The 11/2's insecurities can play out in all kinds of ways—everything from creating emotional enmeshment and drama and wanting to shock whenever possible, to being *so* sweet and *so* nice that others want to puke. The double 1 wants fuel to keep going, and that fuel often comes in the form of admiration and accolades from others. The 2 more commonly feels unworthy or shy about being the center of attention, although the off-track 2 can rival the 1 for self-absorption. A self-absorbed 11/2 can be wildly narcissistic.

A key to balancing the double 1s with the 2 is to step back and take a bird's eye view of how you are engaging with others. If others are coming to you with similar complaints or observations about your behavior and attitudes, you might want to stop and consider the value of their constructive criticism.

"I WISH I WAS SPECIAL"

And you *are* special. The 11/2 knows it's special and that it's here for a reason. And yet, like the song that this little quote is taken from, you might also feel that "I'm a creep. I'm a weirdo. What the hell am I doing here? I don't belong here." Not to be overly dramatic, but 11 is the energy of spiritual illumination. As the Spiritual Messenger, the 11 is regularly reaching into the ethers and coalescing something from that realm into a denser formulation. Bringing ether to *terra firma* can be a bit of a bumpy ride!

The double 1 of the 11/2 is a unique force, and its distinction will get it into trouble every single time it is expressed if it's done only for self-aggrandizement. It does better if it tempers its spiritual activities with the motivation of service that is inherent to the 2. Both the 2 and the 1 share an intense need for approval, as well as desiring recognition for their unique attributes, yet the 2s needs are met primarily through relationships with others while the 1's needs are met by being given space to stand alone and have achievement in the material world.

A WHIRLING DERVISH

The 11/2 has a severe case of ants in the pants. There is so much nervous tension in this vibe that it takes on a life of its own. Blame it on the double dose of initiative, drive, and get-up-and-go. The 2 offers another layer of high anxiety to the 11/2 in the form of worry, self-sacrifice, and people pleasing. Put it all together and you get a walking jolt of caffeine followed by a crash that can mimic a caffeine crash. The 11/2 may be jacked up and jittery one day and then can't roll out of bed the next.

I'd love to say that there's a way to stop the cycle of extreme ups and downs, and yet I find that this will never go away with Master numbers. Ultimately, dramatic energy shifts can only be managed with mindfulness. Interestingly, the 11/2 can come across as somewhat ditzy or absentminded. Given that it can get caught in the ethers, it's no wonder that it takes some concerted effort for it to become grounded.

Observing that the energy of the 11 is intense, in *The Life You Were Born to Live* Dan Millman even suggests that "when inspired or excited, they need less sleep than most people. When they decide to generate something new, inventive, original, or insightful, they have the energy to perform and produce wonders. Their abundant energy is a two-edged sword, however, with great benefits or equally great liabilities."[1] He goes on to observe that the Master 11/2 can have a strong tendency toward addictive behaviors "to discharge a blocked and painful cauldron of constricted creativity."[1]

THE CREATIVE FORCE
OF NATURE

The 11/2 is a dominant creative force of nature. Its creativity can manifest through fine art and performance, or it can show itself in business or family situations. The double 1 brings leadership and innovation and the 2 brings the ability to galvanize people for a common goal, intuitive skills, and a high level of artistic creativity that often shows up in outlets like design, music, and the healing arts.

It sometimes takes the 11/2 a while to recognize and integrate its two disparate halves. Meaning, sometimes it will present much more robustly as a 1 or more distinctly as a 2 rather than as the strange brew that it is. Also, understand that the 11/2 is hypervigilant about its appearance. It's innately concerned not only with how well-liked it is, but also acutely aware of its outer presence. The 11/2 commonly prides itself on looking attractive.

A few snapshots that illustrate key elements of the more optimal presentation of the Master 11/2 can be found in certain traits or in the life stories of Dr. Wayne Dyer and Tony Robbins. Both have Master 11/2 Life Path numbers, and Tony Robbins also has an 11/2 Birthday number as well. Both men experienced abandonment at an early age; Dyer was an orphan living at an orphanage and Robbins' biological father wasn't in the picture and his mother was not mentally balanced enough to offer a safe and secure upbringing for her children. Both men had every excuse and every opportunity to allow their circumstances to define them and to succumb to their challenges by turning to the streets or to any other self-destructive path. Yet somehow, they both listened to an internal voice encouraging them to step into a higher calling, even if they had no idea at the beginning what the calling might be.

Both ended up becoming spiritual teachers and were able to harness and act upon their Master 11/2 purpose as spiritual messengers. Yet we can't minimize the difficult road they experienced as they moved into their roles as conduits for spiritual messages to the masses. Certainly, Dyer spoke freely about his early days where he relied heavily on alcohol. Or Robbins will cite his painful relationship with his mother as a key component to the work he does today. One might also observe that the late Wayne Dyer walked the path of the number 2, learning about love and relationships during his three marriages and by being a father to eight children. Both men are known as innovators. They have certainly embodied the double 1 of the 11 as they have led the way with books, presentations, movies, and many other forms of media through which their pioneering voices can be heard and most people can be reached.

THE CHALLENGES OF THE MASTER

OF THE MASTER

CHAPTER 12

11/2

WHERE IS THE LOVE?

Expressing love is a core mission of any 2, and so it is also a core need for the 11/2. The double 1s bring a self-orientation to the 11/2 that's oppositional to the 2—and often baffling to the 11/2's significant other. Therefore, love and relationships can be rough roads. An 11/2 longs for connection and to love and to be loved, and often has a passion to parent children. The energy of the 1—not to mention the intense master vibe of the double 1 demanding that you step up, lead, and achieve—provides some reasonably high hurdles to jump to attain lasting intimate connections. Because of the 2, having an understanding, supportive, and loving partner is often number one on your list of priorities—so much so, in fact, that at the end of the day success feels empty or devoid of meaning if you don't have someone with which to share it.

Hans Decoz observes that many 11/2s are born into extraordinarily hostile or turbulent families and that their early conditioning results in psychological pain, lack of confidence, and shyness. The life lesson here for the 11/2 is that it sincerely understands the suffering of others and values the importance of close, loving relationships. Its path is often where the 11/2 derives an impetus to devote itself to being of service to others. Decoz goes on to say that "what made you feel weak as a child will make you strong and confident as a mature adult."[1]

"I CAN (CAN'T?) DO EVERYTHING"

Many 11/2s end up forgoing a dream of domestic bliss. Instead they derive love and satisfaction from a career that earns them admiration and respect. Sometimes there's a piece missing for the 11/2 when an ideal intimate relationship hasn't blossomed or the opportunity to have children has passed. I've worked with many 11/2s in the entertainment industry (music, TV, and film) and one of their laments is how they've not been able to cultivate an intimate relationship that feeds their soul. While you don't have to have an 11/2 in your numerology chart for this to be an issue (welcome to the world, right?) —11/2s feel the absence of a soul mate profoundly.

For instance, sometimes an 11/2 performer can have children and identify herself as a mother first, yet she has spent most of her time working on set or on the road traveling to her gigs. Even though she has a heightened sense of pride and purpose in being a mother, if you asked her kids, there would be a gap or a strain in the relationship because of the extended periods of time when their mom was absent. Again, being a working mother isn't good or bad; I am simply making an observation about some of the difficulties 11/2s have expressed as their experience.

There is a skewed sense of self and priority that can come with the 11/2 dynamic and also aspects of "regular" life to be negotiated and resolved. And sometimes that means that long-term marriage or children aren't part of the picture. Or when they are part of your life, you continue to feel inadequate or intensely torn because you have one foot in the domestic realm and the other in the limelight. You may feel as though you are never fully able to put your all into either one.

IF YOU ONLY KNEW

Here's the deal. You'll corner the market on multilayered ego. It typically comes off that you feel misunderstood, out of place, and bristle at the thought of being unnoticed while simultaneously you want to please everyone and be invisible. You want everyone to look at you and yet feel rage when they do—particularly if their gaze is accompanied by any criticism or a snide comment. You want to go first, and your needs surpass all others in importance because you're regularly swimming in the depths of the cosmos. If only everyone could see and understand how acutely your senses calibrate and how expressing yourself is of the utmost importance not only to you but to all creation! You want to be first in line and then feel guilty when you get there, finding someone else to push in front of you who you feel is worthier or in some way needful. Then you resent having placed yourself on the sidelines when the spotlight could have been yours.

You can often mistake sweetness for a means to control and manipulate the people around you. A consistent complaint other people make about 11/2s is that they like to present themselves as so sweet, so giving, and so all-about-you—while underneath it all, everything they do is for their own benefit and has little to do with the ultimate good of the other. The 11/2 can be a smiling manipulator who does its best to kill with kindness. One minute it can be direct and to-the-point (the double 1) and the next moment it can be passive, indirect, and emotionally withdrawn (the 2). The term passive-aggressive encompasses the 11/2. Yet often the 11/2 has no idea that this is how they're operating. They feel they are doing everything for everyone else. Get the idea?

Many 11/2s volley conflicting thoughts and emotions all the time. To volley isn't bad. Its worthy of understanding where some of these contradictory actions stem from so that you can also understand some of the responses and repercussions you may elicit from others.

ILLUMINATION COMES WITH A PRICE

The Master 11/2 has a sense of urgency and volatility. The 11 is the number of *spiritual illumination*, which takes place when darkness or the shadow shows up for a confrontation. Again, remember the opposing elements here: The 1 sets you up for the school of hard knocks, and then the 2 gives you an extreme sense of vulnerability. It may take time for you to get a handle on your ability to identify your emotions and then express them in a healthy way. You can either eat your feelings or use them as weapons.

If you are a Master 11/2, you may have come into the world with such a broad sensitivity to others that you sway from solidly owning your feelings to such an extent that you lose yourself in what you perceive to be the desires and expectations of others. You may also become a belligerent rebel who emphasizes your individuality to the point of self-destruction or self-harm.

While an 11/2 can have self-discipline, it can be challenging for this individual to bring illuminated thoughts and energy down to earth in a productive manner. If this is you, your heart scars easily and you may sometimes feel misused and broken. You may want to put a fence of barbed wire around your heart for protection.

"I JUST GOTTA GET THROUGH THE DAY"

While everyone—no matter what the numbers say—can suffer from addictions, having a Master number in your profile exacerbates the tendency to numb out now and again. Whether it's through soft addictions, like overeating or cigarette smoking, or through a harder addiction, like abuse of drugs and alcohol, you may go through a stage like this before you can come out the other side. Remember that nervous tension we talked about before? This tension is something that can be so disconcerting that you need to dampen it or attempt to control it. And often using substances is the route taken—not to sound too corny—until you discover the magic bullet of consistent meditation, exercise, and other forms of self-care that assist your incredible spiritual potential.

EMBRACING TURBULENCE

The life of the Master 11/2 involves intensely challenging circumstances, so you grow stronger and more spiritually evolved, and become ready to help others who are experiencing similar issues. It isn't easy and yet it's profoundly gratifying when you tap into your high-level of artistic creativity and psychic gifts. Understand that your contribution will be made through the experience you provide for others, which is almost impossible to gauge. You must learn to trust that the butterfly effect you have on people is immeasurable and that you'll never know exactly the way you change people's lives through your loving heart, intuition, and artistic or creative expression. You're the "Wounded Healer" and, as such, must move through a whole gamut of intense experiences.

Understand that you probably won't come into your *full power* as a Master 11/2 until later in life—probably your late forties or beyond. It takes a while to get enough experience under your belt to find your passionate focus. Meanwhile, be patient and know that you're here to offer a higher-level service to the world. It likely won't be a smooth ride, yet it can be amazingly gratifying. You can be a dreamer rather than a doer, so it takes concerted effort to ground yourself in the day-to-day material world. The 11 energy can bring extremism to this dynamic that can be difficult to contain. Part of the challenge of the 11 is learning to align the personal will and sense of being on *terra firma* with divine will or the higher realms.

Those with 11s in their charts will undeniably encounter experiences and situations that are harrowing, difficult, and extreme. The reason for this is because experience isn't just the best teacher, it's the *only* teacher. The person who's mastering the Master 11/2 energy will come through the fire as an inspired healer and wise counselor. But it takes walking the walk and talking the talk to get to the point of mastery.

Actor Robert Downey, Jr., has an 11/2 Life Path and offers a good example of how the intensities the energy of the Master 11/2 can manifest in someone's life. Downey reportedly started taking drugs and drinking alcohol at a very young age. He was brought up in the entertainment industry and started acting early on. His charming and nervous energy was the hallmark of his on-screen personality. Yet most of us remember the mug shot that was splashed on the front pages of magazines when he was arrested on drug related charges. He went to prison, rehab, had a relapse, and another professional comeback. Not only is he apparently sober, his professional career is flourishing again, his private life is more stabilized, and he and his wife have started an organization called Omaze, where he uses his influence to raise money for a variety of charitable causes. His life is an example of the extremes the 11/2 can bring with it, yet when the Master 11/2 comes out the other side, there is great wisdom and positive influence that can follow.

FIVE WAYS TO UNDERSTAND AND INTEGRATE THE MASTER 11/2 ENERGY

CHAPTER 13

GAIN HEALTHY PERSPECTIVE

Gaining a healthy perspective is a hard goal for you to achieve because you *feel* so strongly and so deeply about things. Sometimes the problem is that you create your world as such a frenetic emotional symphony that it's impossible to keep up the tempo and the pace all the time. It's not to your overall benefit to dig into every single teeny-tiny fragment of your emotional landscape or to focus intently on the actions and emotions of other people in your circle or in the world at large. Your gift resides in connecting emotionally with others. In other words, there is a fine line in knowing how to do this successfully without getting overly involved.

You'll tend to push your agenda on others under the guise that you care so very much for them and want to give the sun, the moon, and the stars. And in fact, you have good intentions. But maintaining a posture of caring can result in a hemorrhage of energy and emotion that soon becomes a zero-sum game.

You'll always intuitively be attuned to people and be emotionally supportive of them. The fine line to be navigated in this regard is the line between unhealthy attachment and healthy detachment. You need to learn how to participate and be involved without becoming enmeshed or holding everyone up energetically. When you feel drained, there's a reason you feel drained. It's your inner loudspeaker telling you to stop running after things to fix them and instead let others engage in their own processes. Healthy boundaries and detachment are crucial for the Master 11/2.

EMBRACE YOUR CREATIVITY AND SPIRITUALITY

You're born to be creative and sensitive, yet often it takes several leaps and bounds to come to terms with these broad and vital aspects of your core self. I've known many 11/2s who don't feel creative at all and instead hyper-focus on their family dynamics or their career and job "family." The real challenge of the 11/2 calling is to walk in our world and the world of energy and creation. Every single thing that exists starts as a spark of energy—just a little idea that grows into a thought. That thought somehow comes together enough to be communicated and then manifested as a building, a product, a theory, a machine, or a design. Everything like this comes from the same creative force that the 11/2 can set in motion. The trick is not to get stuck "out there" floating in the limitless ocean of disembodied energy. Visit the energy realm and use it as your source of inspiration, then move into the next phase of development. Allow your ideas to be fully birthed. You're the channel, the conduit, and the space of conception.

YOU'LL RUN THE GAUNTLET

Let's be blunt. Many people with an 11/2 in their chart deal with periods of time when they struggle with extremes. Addictions, accidents, health difficulties, and emotional distress can work their way into the lives of the 11/2. As Tony Robbins (and other motivators and coaches) might observe, the most significant problem with these problems is the idea that you shouldn't have problems. Words from the wise: Tony Robbins has an 11/2 Life Path number and an 11/2 Birthday number. As hard as it is to hear, these types of issues are the cornerstone of your personal power as a Master 11/2. Difficult experiences can initiate you into the club of spiritual mastery.

Think about it. Are there any popular stories about someone born to do something extraordinary where the protagonist has had it easy? Where everything was laid out, simple, and everyone loved them unconditionally and supported their every move? Think of Neo in *The Matrix*. "The Chosen" who has no clue why he's "The One" and bumbles through to fulfill his lofty mission. Luke Skywalker from *Star Wars*. Any of the Marvel superhero movies where superpowers are awkward, uncontrollable, and come with a sufficient amount of sacrifice. I'm a huge fan of the Netflix series *Sense 8* where there is a "cluster" of people who are all psychically connected. Of course, evil forces are hard at work to exterminate them, so their lives are intense and extreme.

You also can go to the stories of the Buddha, Jesus, and other spiritual figures. All were misunderstood and taught outside the conventional wisdom of the age. Of course, the hero's journey is a great thing to read about, yet when it becomes our reality and our own journey where we ourselves must undergo massive challenges, changes, and transformations in our lives, well, that's another story!

Just know that most often the path of the 11/2 has its share of extremity. But you can handle it. And in handling it, you will grow into mastery. Many numerologists observe that often the Master 11/2 vibration brings its share of tumultuousness in the form of health urgencies, accidents, and what might be considered extreme circumstances.

GET FOCUSED

The 11/2 is known as the dreamer rather than the doer. This aspect of the 11/2 paradigm is beautiful and necessary. But there must be a culmination of energy for dreaming to be practical. For thought and vision to manifest through you, you must focus and stay grounded. You will benefit from perfecting skills that allow you to embody and embellish your dreams, views, and ideas as you manifest them. Part of the magic of the 11/2 resides in the unseen energy inherent to the double 1. That energy is most effective when it's balanced by a stabilizing force, and it's up to you to find a point of balance that does the job. Otherwise, the energy of the 11/2 is *too* dreamy, *too* wishy-washy, and *too* non-directed to provide it with optimal effect.

If focusing and being practical are challenges for you, then the next best thing is to bring in someone or something that can ground your energy and your ideas for you. Get help. You can root yourself with the help of an intimate partner or an assistant with whom you have an innate understanding of give and take. Let this individual take care of the nuts and bolts of your ideas while you supply your charisma and vision. There are many ways to focus the highly intense energy of the 11/2 to integrate more efficiently and produce more results in the world. Production starts with having insight about your strengths and weaknesses. Bolster your weakness by capitalizing on your strengths.

LET GO

The power of the number 2 resides in its patience and its powerful trust in divine timing. With the 11/2, this power is amplified. As an 11/2, you have a dynamic combination of patient focus and the ability to engage in right action. It's a profound combination when used optimally. Yet it takes an incredible amount of trust and confidence to let go and surrender yourself to forces that are out of your immediate control or even understanding.

Remind yourself from time to time that all the Master numbers mature like fine wine. With age, wisdom, and experience, the 11/2 gains perspective and can become the master of its emotions. This makes mindful leadership possible. One of the nuggets of wisdom an 11/2 can learn early on is something I remember Oprah Winfrey saying to Brené Brown during an interview. Her basic observation was that to live with integrity, compassion, and healthy boundaries, you must come to terms with the fact that *you will disappoint people*. Brown also observed that in all her years of research she has found that the people who are the most compassionate are also the most strongly "boundaried."[1] They can consistently determine and act upon what's okay with them and what isn't okay. To discern between the two is the key to finding optimal balance with the 11/2.

11:11

CHAPTER 14

The repeating pattern 11:11 has mystical significance and is often referred to as the 11:11 Phenomenon. Whenever we see repeating numbers in our lives—whether they pop up on a digital clock or somewhere else, like on a shopping receipt or a license plate—it's a code signifying an attempt to communicate with us on a different level than the rational, logical way we typically receive communication. It's like the Universe is texting us. The trick we must develop our connectivity and our reception in order to recognize that we're receiving these messages. We need to put the Universe's number in our contact list.

As you know, the 11 is a Master number. What does that mean in this context where you are seeing two 11s? First, remember that the number 1 is all about new beginnings, independence, initiative, achievement, individuation, self-confidence, and innovative creativity. So, when we see this number repeating, it's beneficial to remind ourselves to focus on what we *want* in our lives rather than what we *don't want*—because the energy of the number 1 *expands whatever captivates us and catches our focus*. It's like lighter fluid you spray on firewood to ignite it and get a fire going!

When we see repeating number 1s, it's an indication that a window of opportunity is being flung open. With this energy on our side, we'll begin to manifest our thoughts and desires into reality at turbo speed. It requires us to be disciplined and mindful about how we focus our thoughts. If there's any time to dive into our positive affirmation file, this is the time. Don't waste this valuable and high-powered energy.

As you know, the 11 is the higher-level version of the 2 energy (1 + 1 = 2). The number 2 is all about harmony, balance, cooperation, diplomacy, and love. To this is added the Master number which ups the ante. The 11 is the spiritual messenger. The 11 is highly intuitive, extremely sensitive, out-of-this-world artistically creative, and an inspired healing agent. The 11 lives mostly in the ethers, so an aspect of the struggle with the 11 energy is to bring it down to earth in a way that is useful and constructive rather than diffuse and destructive.

Many believe that when we see the repeating number 11:11 it's a message from the Universe or God, angels, or whatever you believe could be speaking to you from the spiritual realms. When I see this number, I interpret it as the Universe tapping me on the shoulder and giving me a solid "thumbs up!"

A double 11 is an opportunity to enjoy some kudos from universal forces as they acknowledge that we're on the right track. It's beneficial to stop for a moment when you see this number and notice what you're doing right then and there. Exactly what were you thinking? Were you pondering what you were going to have for dinner, replaying the last conversation with your mother when you got angry with her, or are you contemplating a new job?

The 11:11 can appear as an opening—a doorway. If we look at the numbers, we can see this as a visual representation. Each 11 seems like a door. The two doors metaphorically materialize as an intersection between the physical world and the spiritual world. We can be sure that when we see this number sequence we're receiving an affirmation that we're moving forward with our higher purpose in life, even if it doesn't feel like it in the moment.

Sometimes this repeated Master number shows up when we're feeling stuck or unsure about a decision we've been chewing on for a while. Since the 11 is all about spiritual enlightenment, we can use its energy for understanding and manifesting our higher purpose, whatever that might be *right now*. It's an indicator that we're moving forward in a positive direction, like the ultimate spiritual cheerleader. *It's also a message that we must take the right action to achieve what we want to attain.* The 1 is always initiating new beginnings and bold moves forward. It pushes us to take risks and to act.

Have you ever noticed that people who complain all the time seem to have more and more things to complain about every day? Isn't it amazing how so many terrible things happen to complainers? *We attract what we think about on a consistent basis.* Not what we wish we were doing to make our lives better or think others should be doing to make our lives better, but what we continuously think about and allow to occupy our minds. The repetition of 11:11 is reminding us to clean up our thought regimen and clarify our field of intention. The results are amazingly powerful.

When we repeatedly see 11:11, in whatever manifestation or configuration, it's time to focus our intentions on creating and having what we want! This is the best time to focus on a practical plan to get us where we want to go, even if it scares us even to consider that our dreams really could become our reality. We just must really, really, *really* believe that it's possible and then act with conviction on that belief. When people notice this repeating number, often they'll immediately stop what they're doing, take a deep breath, and make a wish or set a clear intention.

Remember, the 11 is our cosmic cheerleader, supportive parent, and universal best friend. Its only purpose for being is to alert us to stay focused and to assure us that we're getting there. So, if you see it, don't waste time and energy lollygagging around. Seeing 11:11 is a window of opportunity that's super-charged—a portal of opportunity for expansion and initiation.

REPEATING NUMBER 1

When you see the repeating number 1, this is a message that you are starting something new and action must occur. It demands that you set clear intentions and focus on what you want to achieve. The 1 always denotes a new beginning, an open door, and a need for a drive, focus, and right action.

PART THREE

22/4

CHAPTER 15

MASTER NUMBER 22/4

"I can talk to all of you, but I can't talk to any of you."
—Jerry Seinfeld

Many numerologists consider the Master 22/4 energy to be the most powerful in numerology. The number 22/4 is a force to be reckoned with when it's refined, disciplined, and well directed. If you have the Master 22 anywhere in your chart, then—on top of the basic characteristics of the number 4 you possess strengths and will confront intense challenges.

To understand what the 22/4 energy may signify for you, it's necessary to be fully aware of the attributes of the number 4. The 4 is the foundational energy at work whenever a 22/4 shows up in your chart, either as your Life Path number or in another location. In this part of the book, we'll go over the number 4 and its meaning first.

Then I will ask you please to go back to the section on the number 2 (see page 67) and read it (or re-read it). Just like with the Master 11/2, the number 2 has a starring role in the makeup of the Master 22/4.

We'll also build our understanding of how the numbers 2 and 4 engage and interact—looking for how they may enhance each other and how they may clash.

As with other Master numbers, the 22/4 is like a sandwich cookie. The 4 is the "filling" and the 2's are the cookies that hold the filling together on both sides!

As a Master 22/4, your unique mission is to execute and build projects that will benefit a vast amount of people. You're a *master teacher* and a *systems builder*. You could also consider yourself a practical idealist. The path of the idealist prods you to step out of the slow, steady security of the number 4 and kick it up substantially. The lack of security in doing so will be uncomfortable until you get the hang of it, as being a leader in this way is contrary to the pull you have with the rule-following, pragmatic energy of the 4.

In *The Life You Were Born to Live*, Dan Millman observes that the 22/4 has "strong tendencies to over cooperate, giving their all and then falling into resentment and withdrawal. Their ambitions can also create blind spots, so they tend to skip necessary steps on the path to their goal. For them, failure is useful feedback if they're paying attention. When 22/4s run into problems, they need to determine which step they skipped and redo it; this releases any pattern of failure. No challenge is too high if 22/4s break it down into small, manageable portions."[1]

You must take into consideration that you're working with the double 2, which is all about harmony, love, and emotional sensitivity, and yet also a 4, which is all about process, stability, and concerted effort. So, there are some special challenges when it comes to fulfilling your mission. You'll be most successful if you use all the hardworking, step-by-step qualities of the 4 while tapping into a higher level of purpose and action. You'll learn to take risks and look toward setting higher stakes with your enterprises. As you're the master builder extraordinaire, look at building solid foundations to your enterprises by always keeping the big picture in front of you. You can institute systems and manifest things in the material realm that can rock the world. You have incredible strength, endurance, and tenacity and when well-directed and focused you can move mountains and effect fantastic change in the world.

The key for the 22/4 is not to go at anything solo! The 22/4 can only reach high levels of success when it brings others on board.

You may not feel up to the task or even entitled to do something that might take you into a significant enterprise—let alone to pursue the path of fame and fortune. You may cringe at the idea of making a lot of money given that the energy of the 4 wants a sense of security—and is not necessarily interested in manifesting wealth. It sounds like a small detail, yet mentally this kind of friction can drag you down.

Bottomline: Avoid your stubborn streak and tendency to be a know-it-all. Gather your supporters around you, set up the systems to make your endeavors work, and hand over some of the responsibilities to others. If you find yourself doing everything yourself, you aren't living up to your Master 22/4 potential.

If you're a 22/4, you're loyal, honest, and methodical and can be easily hurt. The double 2 energy instills you with a hefty dose of sensitivity, but often this sensitivity is kept inside of you where it's not easily read by others. You have high endurance and rival the number 7 in your reasoning and analytical powers. There's a deep drive to accomplish things—both large and small—daily. It's as if you've failed in some way whenever you haven't checked off everything on your punch list each day. Your to-do list is always substantial. "Busy hands are happy hands" was a phrase coined for you.

As a 22/4, you love to devote yourself to projects and to pondering ideas.

You're at your best when you embrace and act upon your practical wisdom and a higher sense of purpose. As a master teacher you have a gift for manifesting amazing things that are meant to change the practical, day-to-day lives of a lot of people. So, ask yourself: "What am I most passionate about?" Pursue something in that arena and dream big. Just know that you're not going to be an overnight success—as if anyone ever is! You're not necessarily set up for luck and ease. Instead, your path involves taking the small, doable steps to build great things and that takes time, commitment, and drive.

With the 22/4, achieving your highest potential is all about learning to break out of your security zone and make an impact on the world around you. Know that this can be somewhat scary and seem foreign to your character because you gravitate toward the tried-and-true and most often err on the safe side. Anytime you hesitate, train yourself to remember: *Master number 22/4 is the most powerful number in numerology.*

Did I just hear you gulp?

Yes. Being a 22/4 is a rather big deal. You're meant to achieve and build something that makes a difference on a grander scale—*and that won't feel comfortable.* If this Master number is in your chart, you must blast past your childhood wounds, through and around your genuine (albeit self-imposed) limitations, and work tenaciously to define and achieve your goals.

Understand that you probably won't come into your full power as a Master 22/4 Life Path until later in life—perhaps your late forties or beyond. It could take a while to get enough experience under your belt to find your passionate focus. Be patient. The result will ultimately be amazingly gratifying.

Periodically you may grapple with an inflated ego or with feeling as though the world is conspiring against you. Grab onto your high-minded ideas and do the long-range planning that it takes to develop an inspired vision. Be ready to act upon your high-level organizational skills and to develop systems of thought and management that carry inspired ideas into manifestation.

Be aware that the sometimes the Master 22/4 can start out on the opposing end of the spectrum—as unmotivated, undirected, and somewhat lazy. If this is the case, the chances are that there will either be a challenging experience that wakes the 22/4 to its correct path or the desire to do more can come to the 22/4 as a sense of a deep inner void and a burning sense that you aren't living up to your potential.

No matter what, you'll be offered more than one opportunity to step into your Master 22/4 power.

The 22/4 is the teacher of teachers. Yet, since this is a part of the mission for the 22/4, there are often issues related to this heightened level of selfless giving.

I have a friend who took a metaphysical course from an instructor who happened to be a 22/4 Life Path. The teacher taught a course where he offered certification for the modality he was teaching. My friend took the course, got the certification, and yet wasn't altogether impressed with the material overall. My friend was happy to take the class and yet she wasn't going to practice *only* these techniques. She was already a coach and while she might certainly integrate some of the material learned from the course (that happened to come with certification), she wasn't using this approach in her coaching business.

She and I were having tea one day and she shared with me her horror when she got a message from the 22/4 instructor berating her for not having the seal of certification from the course on her website and that he was somewhat threatening about wanting to make sure that she was identifying herself as a certified practitioner of his particular modality and giving him full credit.

This is an example of how the Master 22/4 can become single-minded and somewhat off-track with its overall purpose. As a teacher of teachers, the Master 22/4 is here to spread the word. It's almost a stereotype to say that often the student surpasses the teacher—or at least the student learns what they can from the teacher and then takes that knowledge and applies it to whatever they're doing in their own unique way. This is the real mark of success for a teacher and particularly for a teacher of teachers. It's rather like parenting. The point is to prepare students to take the knowledge and make it their own.

Yet when the 22/4 feels as though it has lost control what it considers its proprietary knowledge or when it feels unappreciated or somehow surpassed, then it can extend an enormous amount of energy and effort into attempting to cling to what it considers to be its exclusive "thing" rather than blessing it and casting it off into the world so that it can reach more people and effect more change.

Born July 6, 1935, the Dalai Lama's basic tenets about the infusion of "real life" with spiritual values and the spiritual world are a beautiful example of the Master 22/4 in action. Even though he is a monk and of the highest spiritual calling, as his Holiness the Dalai Lama his message is clear and simple. The primary spiritual values of *love* and *compassion* are always the theme and message that the Dalai Lama speaks of again and again.

In tandem with the Dalai Lama's focus on spirituality, he equally emphasizes rational thought, scientific data, and common sense. As a 22/4 Life Path, the Dalai Lama uses his power and influence to educate people on a grand scale about how to practice and gain spiritual mastery while also living and thriving in the material world. His message is inspired and down to earth, the perfect amalgam of the calling of the Master 22/4.

It may be confusing to understand the meaning of *limitation* when attempting to comprehend the complexities of the Master 22/4. Let's use an example. I have a friend who's a 22/4 Life Path—or a 13/4 Life Path, depending on how you calculate it. He also carries a Master 11/2 as his Birthday number. He's a very spiritual guy with phenomenal psychic abilities. He can read anyone accurately. The trouble is that he himself is a hot mess. Since we're illustrating how limitation shows up, here's how it plays out for him.

Of course, my pal had a challenging upbringing with his family of origin. He couldn't make up his mind about how to decide on a career and went from place to place, from school to school, from job to job—always feeling undervalued, underappreciated, and underpaid.

His choices with relationships were always at the core of his decision making and he went in and out of several rather abusive relationships where he always felt he was carrying the lion's share of the weight despite the fact that he often pushed off financial responsibility to others—either his family or his relationship partners. So, he was always feeling boxed in and limited by his circumstances, yet his circumstances were of his own creation.

Whenever he would finally get out of a bad situation it seemed that he immediately attracted another one. Often the big choices he made—getting married, moving to a different state, quitting a job—were made impulsively and without a plan or much thought about overall consequences. In this midst of all this was drama, drama, and more drama. He would dwell on how his partner should change because he loves him and how dare he not know what he goes through in the relationship. He would quit a job and be unemployed for extended periods of time because nothing was right and yet this made him even more dependent on his partner or strained the family dynamics even further.

In the midst of it all, he would finally make a positive move and then would again act impulsively and sign a lease on a condo that cost far more than he could afford (or something of that nature—making a purchase that was not advisable or practical for the moment), placing himself into a very limited situation financially once again.

While many of these issues are simply things that anyone can go through, if we view them with numerology we can see how certain themes continue to play out. In this instance, this person is working with two Master numbers and the energy of the number 2 (love, relationship, and emotional sensitivity) is paramount in his decision making. Over and over, he opted to entwine himself in relationships rather than take responsibly for himself first.

My friend is extremely intuitive and yet can't harness that gift because he lacks self-awareness and discipline. He makes excuses for the limitations he always creates, which include everything from not having money to health issues. When he settles down for short periods of time he has a remarkable amount of success with whatever he focuses his energies on, yet it's often short lived, and somehow, he can't see that he would benefit from slowing down, setting some long terms goals, and getting real about his life.

Like we did with the Master 11/2, it is beneficial to break down the component of the Master 22/4 by looking at what both the number 2 and number 4 bring to the table.

CHAPTER 16

NUMBER4

AT ITS BEST

A 4's optimal expression is being practical and detail oriented, sharing knowledge, and working to establish a sense of security. Its mission is to develop stability and effective processes. Its purpose is to achieve balance and security by patiently following a gradual plan that carries it toward its goals. It is meant to leave something of lasting value in the world.

THE TORTOISE, NOT THE HARE

The 4 is all about developing stability through the process. This energy isn't rambunctious. Rather, it's cerebral and intelligent, fit for a seeker and cultivator of knowledge. If the 4 were to audition for the cast of *Winnie the Pooh*, it would land the role of Owl—very smart and slightly smug and bossy. Because it knows how to build solid foundations, the 4 usually oversees the development of operating systems and is expected to look after the details. It is the workhorse and "Master Builder" of the world. It also devours information, and there's no end to the depth of its knowledge and ability to impart that knowledge to others. The 4 is a born teacher.

The mission of the 4 is to learn the advantages of systems and order. It will be tempted to skip steps along the way to its objectives, yet when it does, it must go back and make up for those lost steps. This is how it learns to be a master of step-by-step processes. It manifests great things when a goal is articulated, and it maps out steps detailing what it will take to get there.

Someone wrote this comment about the 4 Life Path on my YouTube channel: "Four is boring!" Frequently the 4 gets a bad rap for its supposed lack of humor and having a serious nature. I would argue with that assessment. Fours can be funny. Jimmy Fallon has a 4 Life Path. Chelsea Chandler,

Brad Pitt, Nicole Kidman, and other accomplished celebrities are on the 4 Life Path and I don't find these folks boring. *Au contraire!*

The fact of the matter is that the 4 is learning to be methodical, reliable, and success comes to it when it commits to goals, whatever these may be. Many successful people have 4s in their charts, giving them stamina, practicality, and an incredible drive and ability to work harder than the average person.

LET'S GET CRACKING

The 4 is the number of hard work and concerted effort. A 4's lucky breaks are few and far between. Whatever it takes on requires energy, endurance, and tenacity. It's rare that the 4 finds itself in the midst of something that doesn't need putting in the hours (overtime, anyone?) to get it done. While others are frolicking at the coffee shop behind their computer screens, more than likely the 4 is on its feet behind the counter, out in the field, undergoing training, or any number of other more down-to-earth activities. It's funny about the 4 because often it finds itself wrestling with the oppositional aspects through non-effort, impracticality, and lack of direction. As time wears on, the 4 feels a gnawing sense of unrealized purpose and potential that keeps hounding it until it makes a leap, decides to focus on something, steps it up, gets some systems and routines in order, shows up to the table, and makes a bigger effort. It's all about taking responsibility and getting real.

The 4 can go through phases where it makes every excuse in the book to justify its lack of achievement or its inability to achieve something substantial. But not all 4s start out as slackers.

WEIGHTY ISSUES

Most commonly, a 4 is destined to grow up in the trenches, taking on many responsibilities early on. The 4 must be serious about finances and sometimes misses out on the lighter or more fun elements of life out of this financial necessity. In this way, the 4 is forced to become a realist. Also, know that the 4 can also *choose* to do more serious endeavors as opposed to engaging in the more frivolous aspects of life. It's as though it doesn't have time, energy, or desire to participate in activities that aren't designed to get it somewhere. When others are out partying, the 4 is often found working full time while finishing their degree.

The 4 is built to get results. It tends to be immensely pragmatic and logical. Hard work is a consistent theme because it's learning—while always doing the lion's share of work on a team—how to modulate its efforts. The goal is neither to be a martyr nor a slacker. In their book *Numerology*, Kay Lagerquist and Lisa Lenard observe that "it's the mission of the 22/4 to elevate its body and make it conscious of the oneness of mind, body, and spirit. This number carries the root or reduced, number 4, which governs health. For this reason, it's not uncommon to find 22/4s with weak bodies who have to work on their health, or, at the very least, improve their health using progressive, spirit-honoring methodologies."[1]

CLEAR THE CLUTTER

The number 4 feels most comfortable when moving slowly and deliberately. It thrives on order and organization. Underneath all the planning is a fear of chaos and a real dislike of appearing stupid or naïve in any situation. Overall, the 4 is eminently practical, hardworking, and determined. No matter what, it gets things done. This stability is its superpower.

Think about the how the number 4 looks when drawn on a piece of paper. If you turn the 4 upside-down it resembles a chair—a sturdy surface planted solidly on the ground. That's what the energy is like too. The 4 contributes foundational ideas, products, services, or systems of management to the world. It brings matter into form. It has an earthy energy and thrives when connected, anchored, and grounded through actions and activities having to do with planning and making sure the foundations of things are securely set.

BRING ON THE BOOKS

While the 4 is creative, it usually displays its talents in technical ways. Think photography, calligraphy, playing a musical instrument, any artform that calls for technical skill rather than flamboyant self-expression. Think Ansel Adams, not Jackson Pollack.

A 4 is always absorbing information and seeking knowledge. Overall, it is likely to be a bookworm and someone who subscribes to the Documentary Channel.

The Master 22/4 must grapple with how to integrate and balance the rational practicality of the 4 with the intuition and emotionality of the double 2. Only through the ability and commitment of the energy of the 4 will it bring its gifts and knowledge to fruition. It demands balance coupled with heightened ability to determine the right course of action to usher its ideas into manifestation.

THE ANIMAL WHISPERER

Animals often play an important role in the world of the 4, either as pets/family members or in a broader sense, such as by championing an animal-related organization or cause. The 4 often finds itself president of the local Audubon Society, volunteering for the Humane Society, or adopting a menagerie at home with animals of all kinds. The Master 22/4 can find the unconditional love inherent with animals and pets to offer solace in its hard-working world. It often has an uncanny connection with many elements of the natural world and is able to reduce its stress when enjoying the routine of feeding and caretaking animals.

"DON'T CROSS ME"

The 4 is a protector and prefers things that are tangible, solid, and predictable. Honesty and loyalty are crucial. The 4 is best when doing one thing at a time, not multitasking, as it processes information at a slow and steady pace. Anytime the 4 is pressed to think more quickly or juggle several tasks at once, it will tend to feel overwhelmed. Because it absorbs and processes information at a great depth, the number 4 needs to take plenty of time to cultivate peace. The 4 isn't a big risk taker and often thrives in a more structured and predictable work or family environment.

You don't want to cross the 4. It'll never forget or forgive the infraction, no matter how large or how small. As a rule, the 4 is good at not wanting to argue and then wondering why it is always involved in heated debates with people. The quote "I don't want to argue but let me tell you why I'm right" was made for the number 4.

Underneath everything it does, the 4 has an overweening sense of responsibility and can suffer from stress and nervous tension because of the demands it places on itself.

DRAWING A LINE IN THE SAND

Since hard work is a theme for the energy of the number 4, it can find itself in one of two camps: either taking on much more responsibility than most and being too rooted or avoiding taking on responsibility and putting down roots. My favorite quote from a 4 Life Path: "That's why it's called *work*. It's not *supposed* to be *fun*."

Since work is a constant theme, many 4s have some difficulty connecting with the job or career that genuinely lights them up. It often takes a while for a 4 to get clear on what it wants to do given that *work* ultimately defines how it indeed identifies itself in the world. Fours who don't settle on favorable careers or find a home base for themselves eventually will begin to feel like souls lost at sea. The 4 needs to plant roots and build a stable life for itself, even though it can find this extremely challenging.

The 4 is good energy for architects and people in the construction industry. Anything requiring hard work and endurance also interests the 4. Teaching in any capacity is an excellent fit for the 4. The 4 is also a natural in management positions and thrives within prescribed rules and regulations.

PUT IT ON THE CALENDAR

The number 4 is a stable, steady, and no-nonsense individual. Women with a 4 in their charts may be strong to the point of being perceived as masculine because of having take-charge energy. Super responsible, they take care of everything. Men with a 4 in their charts don't want drama. They want partners who appreciate their ability to provide security.

The 4 isn't one to embrace a lot of change or volatility. At the risk of looking gullible or wrong, the 4 can either trip from similar relationship to similar relationship or opt for staying on the fence. Either way, opening itself to a certain level of vulnerability can prove challenging. The 4 may put on the mask that it has gotten over all of it—an alcoholic ex, an abusive father, an absent mother—and intellectually, that may be true. On a core emotional level, working through difficult and complex family issues is key to the life's work of the 4. The 4 is learning how to create something lasting, reliable, and secure. And doing this isn't something that truly has a finish point. It's an ongoing, lifelong process.

THE FLIPSIDE OF NUMBER 4

CHAPTER 17

"I DON'T WANT TO ARGUE, BUT LET ME TELL YOU WHY I'M RIGHT"

While the 4 can undoubtedly have moments of lightheartedness, it tips the scales toward seriousness and rational thought. The 4 may come off as cynical, arrogant, or holier-than-thou when offering advice, yet what it's trying to do is provide information that will benefit someone or improve a situation. Some might observe that the 4 can have specific superiority issues. It's most often a literal thinker rather than an emotion-based thinker. The 4's the first to say it doesn't want to argue and yet it most usually ends up in arguments because it tends to be opinionated. It needs affirmation and is uncomfortable with—or even afraid of—criticism. If the 4 can't do something perfectly according to its standards, it often won't do it at all. As a result, the 4 ends up in cycles of feeling stuck, limited, and restricted. A 4 can obsess about why "nothing ever works out" or if it does, why it can't work out "more easily." The 4 can make the same mistakes over and over (and over) again—the irony being that its primary goal is not to repeat or ever make a mistake.

"I LIKE MY BOX JUST THE WAY IT IS"

The number 4 is about *limitation*. The 4 energy presents experiences to us when it appears in our charts that show us how we limit ourselves and—in turn—how to move through (around or over) constraints. Given that this is a theme for the vibe of the 4, it offers ample opportunities to come face to face with limiting circumstances, whether these are physical, mental, emotional, spiritual, financial, or a combination of the above. As a result, the 4 person is known for being more of an inside-the-box thinker who benefits from rising above the water line and seeing that there are other ways of thinking and operating.

The 4 is the ultimate micromanager. Only when it steps out of its way can it truly have success. Although it has the gift of knowledge-based and systematic thinking, it needs to soften and massage some of its rigidity into flexibility. The 4 craves structure and security, yet these things need to be balanced and modulated or else they become barriers.

SECURITY AT ANY COST

Home is important for the 4. It craves a sense of security that the idea of a home exemplifies. One of the primary issues the 4 brings to the mix is the necessity to work through issues with its family of origin. While all of us have family history to deal with, the 4 rides a particularly rough or intense road with its family that is at the core of the healing and learning it has come here to do. If someone experiences the energy of the 4 during a cycle of time, issues related to old emotional wounds are bound to come up.

To work optimally with the gifts of the 4, its beneficial to look at wounded, dysfunctional, or otherwise problematic relationships and work through the feelings of lack and pain they create. Often a 4 will staunchly assert that they're over their family issues and yet they still occupy a lot of the 4's emotional energy. It's a matter of truly coming to terms with the pain and letting it go sincerely. Of course, all human beings benefit from healing their personal trauma. It's just that this is a foundational theme when the energy of the 4 is at play.

DOWN DOG, ANYONE?

There is a definite tendency for the 4 to develop somewhat rigid or black-and-white rules for life that it feels everyone should adhere to, respect, and follow. The 4 is baffled by people who can't plan, don't follow the rules, and live more in the emotional realm than it does. *These people just need to get real, get with the program, and get a life, right?* The 4 is optimized when it surrounds itself with people who push it just a little bit out of its comfort zone and encourage it to take calculated risks.

The number 4 has strict ideas about "right and wrong," "good and bad," and "acceptable and unacceptable." The more rigid these thought patterns become, the less flexible its body becomes. A 4 often suffers from lower back issues and headaches as a result. It's therefore imperative for the 4 to engage in both physical and mental activity that loosens and supports flexibility on all levels.

BRINGING THE DOUBLE 2 INTO THE 4

CHAPTER 18

The Master number 22/4 brings the double 2 into partnership with the number 4. Remember, a person with a Master number in their chart can feel like a Siamese twin with two entirely different brains attached to one shared body. Combining the two identities is the magic, beauty, and harrowing journey of the Master number. In this case, it's useful to conceptualize the Master 22/4 as two parts 2 and one part 4.

Here are five suggestions for introducing the number 2 to the number 4 so that they become fluid and powerful dance partners.

"ME, SENSITIVE?"

The 4 can present as coolly rational and emotionally disengaged. With the 22/4, the double 2s tend, however, to override the levelheadedness that the 4 brings to the table. The inherent imbalance of the paired energy ensures a beautiful convergence of the yin and yang of intuition and practical application, of knowledge and emotion.

If you are a 22/4, the issue can be that others can't see just how sensitive you are and you can feel wounded when they don't pay attention to your deep feelings. Part of that lack of attentiveness comes from the tough outer shell that you often display. The 4 is, after all, pragmatic and doesn't have time to frolic or for folly. You may be perceived as someone who doesn't get his feelings hurt very easily because you announce this fact, even when you really do. Your incredible strength, stamina, and ability to reason can be decoys to keep you safe as you routinely grapple with your deep emotional sensitivity.

In *The Life You Were Born to Live*, Dan Millman notes that the temperament of 22/4s "swings from over-accommodating to resistant" and that "they aren't always inclined to compromise or to listen to others' feedback."[1] Overall, the 22/4 can accomplish anything it sets out to do as long as it is willing to take small, manageable step to get there and keeps an open mind in the process. Given that the 22/4 is often jacked up and stressed out, an essential element for its success is to develop a mind/body/spirit regimen that encourages relaxation and reduces stress on every level. Only then can the 22/4 be fully open to be a catalyst for revealing its great enterprises.

DO UNTO OTHERS

One of your challenges, if you are a 4, is that you can be a bulldozer, plowing through every situation without real consideration that there are others to contend with and consider. Because you've done your homework, stayed up late doing the research, and have a logical, pragmatic way of viewing the world and diving into solving a problem, you have strong opinions about how things should be done and have little patience for those who disagree. The power of the 2 resides in your ability to see all sides of the equation—to understand opposing points of view and mediate winning outcomes by keeping the good of the whole in mind at all times.

The 2 is the mistress or master of patience, whereas the 4 is impatient—or at least has little time or energy for veering away from the current goal. Interestingly, the 22/4 can be extremely impulsive—just the opposite of its Master calling. This impulsive, or even compulsive, behavior can result in excessive worrying and overall regrets about steps taken and not taken. Millman says that "22/4s have strong tendencies to over-cooperate, giving their all and then falling into resentment and withdrawal. Their ambitions can also create blind spots, so they tend to skip necessary steps on the path to their goal . . . When 22/4s run into problems, they need to determine which step they skipped and redo it; this releases any pattern of failure."[2]

WHY CAN'T IT BE EASIER?

Both the 2 and the 4 can get carried away with their sense of duty and responsibility. The 2 feels responsible for keeping the peace and making sure everyone is happy while the 4 feels accountable for tasks being orderly and completed. So, when you put them together—and leave them unchecked—the tunnel vision that occurs can make many aspects of life feel overwhelming or insurmountable.

In *Numerology*, Kay Lagerquist and Lisa Lenard observe that "a lot of Master Number people don't live up to their spiritual potential. In part, it's because it's so hard to live life as highly sensitive individuals—and they must live in balance. This requirement to balance extends to the physical, emotional, and mental aspects of their lives, and, quite frankly, it's a tall order."[3] The methodical nature of the 4 joined with the detail-driven nature of the 2 offers powerful energy with which to get things accomplished—yet not without the angst that comes with attempting to achieve great things in an overall sea of mediocrity.

The 22/4, like the solo 4, must navigate the healing—or at least the deep investigation—of its relationship with its parents and siblings. While everyone experiences some dysfunctional family dynamics, because this is such an integral aspect of the overall purpose of the 4 it is extended on an intensified level to the 22/4.

LEAVE IT TO ME

One of the key issues for all Master numbers is the spiritual task to stay in alignment with, and not abuse, the power that comes with the Master number. It's one thing to have lofty goals and another to pursue those goals with the only motivation being self-aggrandizement. All Master numbers point in the direction of sacrifice, compassion, and service on some level. The 22/4 can rival the 8 in its tendency to become a workaholic and over focus on achievement at all costs. In her book *Numerology*, Juno Jordan makes the point that there is a "strange inner conflict" for the 22/4 insofar as "the 2 finds it difficult to bring its thoughts and desires down to the ordinary everyday activities and to put into *form* and *order* its concepts and finer attributes. The 22 often needs the help and support of others and must learn to cooperate with circumstances—not pull *against* them. Often there is a dominant person in the environment to test the peacemaking qualities of the 2, causing the 22 much unhappiness and sorrow."[4]

LET ME EXPLAIN IT TO YOU

The interplay between the double 2 and the 4 can turn into heightened bluntness or exaggerated victimization. One of the significant adverse attributes that can come up with the 22/4 is the avoidance of life's possibilities and responsibilities. Yet on the road to nowhere, the 22/4 can get mired in an obsession for telling others what to do and how to think. This condescending attitude can become an overwhelming self-imposed "job" for the 22/4.

Dan Millman has observed that the 22 can "always seem to verge on the edge of one crisis or another. They are frequently frantic, even hysterical. They experience inner confusion and stress. Making impulsive decisions they later regret, they stubbornly hold their course and repeat the same mistakes. Their forceful, rigid views create anger when others don't do what these individuals think they should. As master codependents, they overgive to the point of depletion. They form intense relationships, which they throw themselves into at first and then cut themselves off from, feeling alienated and resentful. Generally impatient, they want to get everything done *now*, without going through the necessary step-by-step process."[5]

The power and the beauty that both the 2 and the 4 can manifest is magnificent when used and managed optimally. The sensitivity of the 2 working in tandem with the 4 can produce reliable, tangible results.

THE CHALLENGES OF THE MASTER

CHAPTER 19

22/4

TAKE ME TO THE LIMIT

Numerologist Hans Decoz points out that the existence of the 22/4 is rife with frustrations and disappointments. These frustrations often have to do with internal limitations—such as limiting belief patterns—and restrictions based on external factors—such as health problems, geography, and other issues. The 22/4 is the Master Builder, not a speedy magician! Often it would like to see things happen with more immediacy and this is rarely the case. The 22/4 encounters more in the way of hardship and a need for concerted effort than the average person.

I've never met a 22/4 who didn't feel as if they deserved a break and yet never get one. Or if they did get a break, the relief was short-lived and ultimately insubstantial. Often the 22/4 experiences a base-level feeling of exasperation and exhaustion that's tough to shake off. Remember, this is a powerhouse energy. As a Master number energy, it brings with it nervous tension and feelings of needing to build something big or of lasting value. The double 2 adds double the emotional sensitivity to the practical 4. So, there's volatility involved here that confounds the 22/4. There is a strong internal feeling that there is something important to be done and only you can do it—and you think it should have been done yesterday!

UNDER PRESSURE

The ego of the 22/4 is different than the ego of the 11/2. Because of the double 1, the 11/2 is self-oriented with a soft center representing the 2. The 22/4, by contrast, brings in double the energy related to wanting to love and be loved in return.

The 2 also brings heightened intuition, emotional sensitivity, and conflict avoidance.

The foundational power of the 4 is emotionally detached, lodged in rational thought and practicality, and has little patience for emotional quagmires. And usually the 4 is anything but conflict avoidant. Confrontation, anyone? Bring it on! So, because of the double 2, the 22/4 is a strange mix, volleying between emotional sensitivity and a just-get-it-done attitude. The collision of the energy of the 2 and the 4 manifests as someone with a know-it-all presentation who often has difficulty dealing with people who aren't on the same page. Unlike the airier 11/2, the 22/4 means business and is all about getting the work done. It requires a plan, a calendar, and a deadline.

If you look at the numerology charts of people who are considered achievers in the world, you'll see that a 4 or multiple 4s often show up. The 4 gives us stamina, drive, and endurance. This energy is necessary to manifest something on *terra firma.*

While 11/2s are channels for higher ideas and ideals, they often can't bring their ideas or ideals into practical reality without the assistance of people possessing more grounded energy. By contrast, 22/4s are light on creative ideas and heavy on the ability to systematize and bring things to life, whether those things are their ideas or someone else's. Often the 22/4 is best at taking something that already exists (for example, a product, a service, a design) and developing and expanding upon it.

GUMBY IS YOUR FRIEND

The Master 22/4 has a sense of urgency and volatility. Again, remember the effect of the opposing elements here: The 2 gives you emotional sensitivity and a rather extreme sense of vulnerability. The 4 makes you more of a go-to guy or gal. You're the solid, steady, *get 'er done* person and must have a punch-list of accomplishments by the end of each day to feel on task. One of the trademarks of the Master 22/4 is a sense of dogged adherence to rules and to what you consider to be the right way to do things.

When I say *rules,* I don't necessarily mean *the* rules as established by authorities—although it can mean that kind of rule following. What I mean is *your* rules—those which you determine to be sacrosanct.

Once you dig your heels in, you're immovable. Sometimes this is to your benefit, as you can work with tenacity and persistence to get through obstacles that would make others weep and run away. Sometimes digging your heels in is to your detriment, such as when you overlook newer or different avenues of thinking, problem solving, or doing things overall.

Often 22/4s take great pride in being the best at whatever it is they do—and then spend an inordinate amount of time being upset when others don't meet their standards or give them the accolades they deserve for their expertise. They just feel that people should perform at a certain level defined by their standards. I had one friend who used to drive another 4 Life Path friend of mine insane when he'd goad her with this statement. "Rules are just suggestions with consequences." To the 4, rules are rules, not suggestions.

If you're a 22/4, know that inflexibility can adversely impact your physical wellbeing. The 22/4 should be mindful about nurturing the body with a balanced exercise regimen that includes rigorous cardio (if possible), flexibility (yoga, Pilates, and stretching), and suppleness of mind cultivated through meditation or any form of relaxation technique that works for you.

Actress Kristen Bell said something that pertains to the challenging elements of the number 4 when she shared something her therapist told her. "Honesty without tact is cruelty."[1] Often the 22/4 can speak bluntly and without a filter—and even though often the observations can be correct, the 22/4 may seem cruel in conveying their opinions to others.

DETOURS

While everyone—no matter what their numerology—can suffer from addictions, having a Master number present in your profile exacerbates the tendency to go through periods of time where you opt to numb out. Whether it's through indulging soft addictions, like cigarette smoking, or harder addictions, like drugs and alcohol, often you go through a stage of self-medication. Remember that nervous tension we talked about before? This sensation is something that can be so disconcerting that you may feel a need to dampen it or attempt to control it. Often substance abuse is the route taken—not to sound too corny—until you discover the magic bullet of consistent meditation, exercise, and other forms of self-care that cultivate your incredible spiritual potential.

One of the downsides to the energy of the 22/4 is that it's often a proving ground for achieving long-range plans and goals. It's a path where there will be more than your share of frustrations and disappointments along the way—enough to drag anyone into the muck. It's not a casual ride or a frolic based on impulse. Challenges with tapping into an innate sense of satisfaction and contentment rather than a constant state of anxiety or discontent measure the 22/4's path. Part of this is this consistent feeling that you're behind the eight ball and have "got to, got to, got to." "I've *got* to finish that task. I've *got* to call her back. I've *got* to prepare for the meeting. I've *got* to do his part of the project that he didn't do right. I've *got* to make sure it's all perfect." It's a delicate balance to offer yourself the space, breaks, and time for some lightness or fun along the way when the demands of the world seem to rest directly, and heavily, upon your shoulders.

REPEATING NUMBER 2

When you see the repeating number 2, this is a message about love, connection, and all things in the relationship realm. A 2 indicates a need for patience and assures you that when you use patience, you will reap rewards. Diplomacy is necessary. You can anticipate receiving the benefits of partnership either business or in love. Remember to seek support and focus on love.

REPEATING NUMBER 4

When you see the repeating number 4, this is a message about the manifestation of your intentions. The ephemeral is becoming material. This code indicates that what you're working on is going to come to fruition. Universal forces are supporting you and helping your enterprises grow and blossom. A 4 is a sign to continue to work with tenacious focus. When you do that, you will gain momentum and cosmic assistance. It is a good idea to ask your universal support team for help and thank them for what they've previously helped you to achieve. With organization, effort, and clarity of purpose, you will meet or surpass your expectations.

FIVE WAYS TO UNDERSTAND AND INTEGRATE MASTER 22/4 ENERGY

CHAPTER 20

BUSINESS AS USUAL

Both the numbers 2 and 4 are "business" numbers. Numerologist Glynis Mc-Cants observes that the 2 is in the business of love and relationship while the number 4 is in the business of stability and security. Together they make a solid relay team, one that stands out for its more serious nature. There is an innate drive with Master 22/4 to be a player behind the scenes, to take on the details, and to serve as the point-person for projects and relationships. The integration comes when the emotions-based 2 can hold hands with the more practical nature of the 4.

Part of the conundrum of this Master number depends on what the 22/4 chooses to expose and what it keeps locked away inside. Most often the 22/4 will err on the side of caution and therefore it can have a difficult time coming to terms with and integrating its softer, intuitive side and its emotion-based side. The energy of the 22/4 is practical and logical. It thrives on predictable routines and the clarification of tangible goals. But the energy here becomes amazingly powerful when it successfully integrates its business-minded nature with the intuitive and loving energy of the 2.

GET OUT OF YOUR WAY

The life of the 4 is rife with difficulties and challenges related to limitation. Mixed with the default mode of the 2, which is to overgive to the point of withdrawing with resentment, then you have a real party on your hands! The trick is to harmonize the power of the 22 with an ability to step out of your own way and stop micromanaging wherever in your life you tend to do so—which is probably in most aspects!

One of the primary hurdles for the 22/4 is to bring judgment to a minimum while still moving steadily toward what it wants. With the 22/4, you can easily get sidetracked by doing things because you think it's expected of you or is a requirement. You'll experience more than your share of problematic family dynamics related to limiting belief patterns and behaviors. It can take a while for you to hone in on what you really want to do.

MENTAL, PHYSICAL, AND EMOTIONAL EXHAUSTION

The 22/4 is in it for the duration, and that requires pacing, training, and stamina. It often finds out the hard way that it can't do everything itself—and if it does, it pays the price. I don't know a 22/4 who hasn't experienced periods of depression and burn out. This can show up as health issues, accidents, or anything that keeps its physical body from performing as it expects it to perform. The tendency is for the 22/4 to push through and work harder and harder and harder—although hard work doesn't yield better results. You can only do so much single-handedly. The task for the 22/4 is to loosen the grip, stop being a one-woman or one-man show, and bringing others on board to help out. Even so, it's strangely tricky and counterintuitive for the 22/4 to seek support and usually this unwillingness to be dependent on supporters stems from a genuine lack of support received early in life. Basically, there's a need for the 22/4 to unlearn aspects of childhood that continue to hold it hostage, even if originally this individual learned to do it all alone out of survival and self-protection.

If you're a 22/4 and you opened to your intuitive abilities early on, you know that you don't quite fit the mold. As you develop and pursue your Master mission, you must grow to trust others and open yourself to communicating your needs, desires, and ideas to others.

Often the 22/4 can rival the number 7 in its desire to carve out substantial alone time. The 4 energy that is its foundation craves a sense of peace and order that is wholly and completely self-contained and self-controlled.

TIME TO LIGHTEN UP

The 4 corners the market on overall seriousness. There's work to be done, after all, with no room for slacking or wasting time. And while the "get 'er done" attitude of the 4 is generally a great attribute, sometimes people just don't get why it's so severe in the 4's case. *Why can't he/she just chill out and have a little fun once in a while?* they wonder.

If you're a 22/4, there's often pressure associated with your engagements. It is as if you're always checking your watch (metaphorically speaking) and making sure you're getting through your neverending punch list. Even when you're involved in what might be considered fun activities, you may feel a need to make sure the goings on are meeting the mark in terms of what you think to be the rules and regulations. You tend to criticize when things don't measure up to your standards, whether that's how people are behaving at a party (badly), what someone says (what an idiot), or how stupid and ineffective the system is and how you could make it better (if others only had a clue).

TRY SOMETHING NEW

One of the caveats to the energy of the number 4 is that—*overall*—it cringes at the thought of dealing with something new. The tried and true is what the number 4 thrives upon. It has a deep need for order, organization, stability, and a clear sense of right and wrong. The 4 needs a support system that will push it to open its mind a little more and step off the beaten path. If you have other more creative numbers in your overall chart, this can be a point of balance and integration for you. If not, this can be more of a challenge. Particularly with the calling of the Master 22/4, the 4 needs encouragement to take a few calculated risks and embrace the higher calling that comes with the Master number. Yet this means that the 22/4 is required to move through fear and resistance to change. More than other numbers, this combination demands that you get out of your own way and you'll have to practice this again and again.

As a 22/4, you'll benefit most from actively and consciously cultivating relationships that support you and encourage you in stretching outside of your comfort zone.

PART FOUR

33/6

CHAPTER 21

MASTER
NUMBER
33/6

"Don't dig up in doubt what you planted in faith."
—Elizabeth Elliot

If you have the Master number 33 anywhere in your chart, then you'll have greater strengths and more intense challenges than the standard 6. When you have a 33/6, it's necessary to be fully aware of the attributes of the 6, which is the foundational energy at work in your chart. You also need to become familiar with the 3 and its meaning. Master 33/6 is a high-octave energy that is challenging to modulate and is extraordinarily powerful.

The 33/6 is a "newer" Master number insofar as many numerologists didn't consider it in reading charts until recently—meaning, during the last several decades. People with 33s in their charts are fewer than those with 11s or 22s, so the discussion about its attributes and challenges can be difficult to illustrate. Many numerology software programs don't calculate the 33. So, if you're concerned or curious whether there is a Master 33 in your chart or the chart of someone you care about, do the calculations manually. Let's look at the attributes of the number 6, which provides the foundational energy at work when you show a 33/6 as your Life Path number or whenever it shows up in any other location in your chart.

In this part of the book, we'll first go over the number 3 in its optimal state and on the flipside, then we'll consider how it relates and potentially conflicts with the energy of the number 6. As with our other Master numbers, the 33/6 is like a sandwich cookie. The 6 is the "filling" and the pair of 3s hold the filling together on both sides!

As a Master 33/6, your mission is to be a masterful healer or teacher, an inspired visionary, and a conduit for unconditional love. The combination of these two numbers indicates yours is a spiritual path. Like others with Master numbers in their charts, this energy will prod you to tap into your creativity and emotions and engage in nurturing and healing service to others. Blending two parts 3 and one part 6 in a blender with other ingredients, the cocktail could come out in different ways. How you use and embody your 33/6 energy will be unique to you—and depends on the rest of your chart. Even so, we can expect that the energy produced will be a potent blend of joyful, loving, creative, and responsibility driven tendencies. Your destiny is as a Master Teacher.

In *The Life You Were Born to Live*, Dan Millman asserts that "those on the 33/6 life path are here to work through issues of perfectionism, emotional expression, and self-doubt to bring forward their inspiring vision of life's possibilities while appreciating the innate perfection of the present moment."[1]

Remember, you're a double 3—and the 3 is all about creative expression and emotional sensitivity—and yet inherently a 6—a number that's all about nurturing, acceptance, and vision. You'll experience the challenges related to both these numbers and fulfilling your life's purpose may be particularly challenging. It's a big calling, which is sure to fall into one or more of the selfless, helping, healing, and creative realms. The number 33 is known by some as the "Christ number." Nothing daunting about emulating that, right?

Hans Decoz suggests that 33 indicates the highest form of "divine realization" and says that the ultimate gift of the 33 is its extraordinary teaching abilities. He also maintains that the extreme nervous tension of people sharing this Master number often manifests as severe insecurity.[2]

In *Master Numbers*, Faith Javane suggests that both sacrifice and sincere concern for others is part of the path for the Master 33. She also observes that:

Those born under Master number 33 are outgoing and giving of themselves in service to others. A keen sense of duty and justice underlies their conduct. They attempt to help reform those who indulge in harmful actions. They try to answer the hunger for spiritual truth and make it satisfying to the masses. They strive to show this by setting an example of love and forgiveness in all their dealings. They minister selflessly to all who seek their aid. These individuals spend their entire lives in devoted service.[3]

The 33/6 is exceptionally talented and has a powerful connection to the spiritual realms when it is open to stepping into this higher calling. Love is the resounding theme for the 33/6, and it's the birthright of anyone walking the path of the 33/6 to be an evolved spiritual teacher. The 33/6 must learn to develop a certain level of humor, lightheartedness, and cheerful disposition to counterbalance the more substantial and despairing elements of the world.

The implication of having Master numbers in your chart is that you must develop and refine the energy over time—the process is comparable to aging fine wine or cheese. *The 33/6 energy demands that you must—first and foremost—heal yourself.* With that in mind, understand that you'll be put into situations that require that you practice dealing with responsibility. Your job is to learn to take responsibility for yourself and your actions while not becoming a martyr, enabler, controller, or meddler. Do not unduly accept responsibility for the duties of others.

The power of the 33/6 isn't easy to master or modulate. It can manifest under different conditions. Wherever it shows up for you, if you have a 33/6 in your chart, the abstract concept is the same: *It's your calling to teach, and to show by example, the power of unconditional love.* Having a Master number of any kind presupposes that you'll take on leadership positions. The 33/6 encompasses visionary goals, truth, beauty, justice, and a nurturing and giving heart. Optimally, the 33/6 is a bright and shining presence whose vision and enthusiasm is contagious.

There are 33/6s who are police officers, wives, mothers, doctors, or work behind the scenes at their churches and temples. There are many 33/6s in the entertainment industry, as its activities are underscored by highly charged artistically creative energy. No matter which industry you work within, you can fulfill your mission by visiting retirement homes, hospice organizations and other agencies, and by somehow offering yourself to those in need of solace. You could be the wealthy philanthropist who opens the new wing at the local cancer center and provides holistic services there which were not offered before. You could be a nurturing spouse, parent, or community service leader, or just the best and most reliable friend on the planet. There are countless ways that you will act upon your 33/6 master energy.

Interestingly, it's more challenging to discern a "true" 33/6 than an 11/2 or a 22/4 because a 33 is a rarer occurrence in a chart than an 11 or 22. For instance, let's look at the actress Meryl Streep's information. Her birthdate is June 22, 1949. Notice also that she has a Master 22 as her Birthday number.

So, we can add it the proper way:

June = 6

22 = 22 (as a Master number, the 22 is not reduced)

1949 = 1 + 9 + 4 + 9 = 23

2 + 3 = 5

6 + 22 + 5 = 33

Now, if you disagree with the school of thought that the Master number should not be reduced, then you will do your calculation as follows:

$6 + 4 + 5 = 15$

$1 + 5 = 6$

Or added together:

$6 + 2 + 2 + 1 + 9 + 4 + 9 = 33$

So again, we can see how the mode of calculation will offer different outcomes in determining whether a Master number is present.

The Master 33/6 is a high-level calling that often reveals itself in the trenches. I read a news story about an incident where a young man was robbed and killed walking home from the grocery store. The young man who killed him was only fourteen years old and he was caught and convicted of the murder. The story revolved around the mother of the murder victim.

In court, her amazing show of strength and grace touched each and every person in that courtroom and beyond. Instead of a display of rage and vengeance, when sentencing was delivered in the courtroom, this mother walked over to the perpetrator and hugged him. She told him she forgave him. She said that she would always be a part of his life because of his actions and she wanted to help him forgive himself and get his life on track. While I have no idea what the numerology chart is for this woman, her act of extreme unconditional love in the face of all odds is what I consider the theme for the Master 33/6. It's the force of unconditional love acted out as an example for others—most often under rather intense or extreme circumstances.

Actor Peter Dinklage (whose numerology chart is referenced on page 48) exudes the depth and charisma indicated by his multiple Master numbers. As a 33/6 Life Path, he certainly contains and shares the wisdom of this higher calling. In a commencement speech at Bennington College in 2012, Dinklage tells the story of how he walked away from his soul-crushing job as a data processor in order to pursue his calling as an actor. He observes:

I tell this story because the world might say you're not allowed to yet. Please don't even bother asking. Don't bother telling the world you are ready. Show it. Do it. Trust me, the rhythm sets in. Just try not to wait, like me, until you're 29 before you find it. And if you are, that's fine too. Some of us never find it. But you will. I promise you. Raise the rest of your life to meet you. Don't search for defining moments, because they will never come. The mo-

ments that define you have already happened. And they will already happen again. Don't wait until they tell you you're ready. Get in there. I waited a long time out in the world before I gave myself permission to fail. What did Beckett say? 'Ever tried, ever failed. No matter. Try again. Fail again. Fail better.' The world is yours. Treat everyone kindly. And light up the night.[4]

One might observe that he was dealt a challenging hand of cards being born a "little person" into a world where certainly this has been seen as a "condition" or a "disability." The lessons provided by the Master numbers sometimes involve this type of journey where there are quirks and differences that offer both challenges and—when embraced—*strength.*

NUMBER 3

CHAPTER 22

AT ITS BEST

A 3's optimal expression is dynamic, self-assured, joyful, emotionally balanced, and inspiring. Its mission is to develop itself creatively, hone its emotional sensitivity, and perfect the art of communication. Its purpose is to use these traits to heal itself and to inspire and uplift others.

"I'M READY FOR MY CLOSEUP"

The 3 is born to perform on center stage. It loves creativity, communication, and connecting with people. It communicates brilliantly and clearly because it consolidates information efficiently. It's a master at knowing intuitively how to rework knowledge and generate new ideas and solutions. The 3 embraces its creative impulses with gusto. Overall, it can make someone the life of the party—clever, witty, the clown, entertaining, charismatic, and good company. This is the easygoing host who makes people feel nurtured, relaxed, and comfortable. Often the 3 directs its creative skills and talents to a select area, such as theater, film/TV/broadcasting, dance, cooking, music, photography, speaking, writing, or coaching. It is naturally inclined toward the arts and other modes of expression that can serve as conduits for its effervescent energy and unbridled creativity. Some people would label the 3 as quirky or unusual as it infuses creativity into solving or managing whatever task is at hand.

"LET ME BE CLEAR"

Since its life purpose relates to communication, the 3 will be asked to hone and perfect its communication skills every day in every way. In conversation, it's usually direct and compassionate, and yet if it's still developing these skills, it could tend to become domineering and state its thoughts and feelings bluntly, which can be hard on those on the receiving end.

Truthfully, the 3 often works long and hard to identify that it even has beliefs or opinions. If this is the case, its communication is rudimentary at best or nonexistent at worst.

Whether it is a good communicator or a poor communicator, *communication* is an ongoing theme.

At times, the 3 may default into sarcasm and inappropriate humor. It can talk all the time while saying absolutely nothing. Or it makes everyone in the room grimace with off-color jokes and improper remarks.

On the other end of the spectrum, a 3 may never communicate anything at all. It clams up and fails to express thoughts, opinions, and emotions and then wonders why it never experiences emotionally satisfying relationships. Just know that the 3 sometimes goes through periods of stunted communication where it can, for instance, be great at communicating in some places (such as on the job) and yet in other places (such as in it family or friendships) it's constrained.

IT'S ALL GOOD

The 3 is indeed the energy of *joie de vivre* (the joy of life). Part of its function is to appreciate and express the pure joy of living. Sounds easy, right? Its ability to comprehend and communicate this joy is one of the many ironies of the 3 because it also can struggle to find the lightness amid the substantial quantity of emotional energy it experiences and processes. One of the primary goals for the 3, therefore, is to see and engage with the lighter elements of life and bring joy and optimism to everything it experiences. Ultimately, it is here to inspire and uplift others by tapping into deep core emotional elements.

The power of the 3 resides in its ability to fully experience all emotions without filtering out any of them—the good, bad and the ugly—and gaining pearls of wisdom in the process. It gains wisdom by delving deeply into the emotional crevices. When confronting periods of darkness or crisis, it must learn to come through them with humor, good grace, and healthy discernment. The 3 is here to learn to speak its truth, find joy, and create. As it does this, its effect on others will have glorious ramifications. It can serve as an example to others of how to move through adversity while smiling—and not in a saccharine or fake sort of way, but in a real and profound way.

RIDING THE WAVES OF EMOTION

Many constructive aspects of the 3 are derived from its connection with its emotions—and it seems to have a lot of them. If emotions were colors, we could say that its palette is vibrant and dynamic.

In the same way the 3 has to learn that it even has opinions, the 3 may need to spend years to be able to gauge that it even *has* feelings and how to express them. The 3 is so closely attuned to the emotions of others (rivaling the 2 in this way) that it often doesn't realize the extent that it picks up emotional flotsam and jetsam from the environment around it. Until it can get a handle on what is its own and what belongs to everybody else, it's destined to carry emotional debris around with it in an overloaded emotional backpack.

The 3 can present itself to others as stoic, failing to acknowledge emotions in any way, shape, or form. Fortunately, this doesn't have to last long. As soon as there is a significant crisis, the emotional center can break wide open. The 3 can spiral out of control, exaggerating and accentuating every fragment of emotional engagement to the point of exasperation. The goal for the 3 is to learn to embrace emotions, experience them, and move through them fully and completely.

A QUICK WIT AND INTELLECT

The energy of the 3 is vital, curious, and buoyant. It gets easily frustrated and feels impatient with those who can't keep up with its lightning-fast thought processes. It's the birthright of the 3 to experience, dabble, and study a wide variety of subjects. However, the 3 also must ultimately take all of that information and create something unique with it. Its highest and best use is when it can settle on bringing something (or a focused combination of things) into practical reality. The 3 can experience defeat and frustration if it feels it has nothing to show for itself. Optimally, it must commit to going past superficial knowledge and digging deeply enough to become an expert in its chosen field.

If the 3 is worried about disappointing someone by doing what it is called to do (as opposed to doing what someone else wants it to do), it can quickly become a jack-of-all-trades and the master of none. One of the pressures of the 3 is that it's so good at everything it does that it has a hard time choosing a singular focus. The 3 is known to be scattered and easily distracted—not to mention quickly overwhelmed. The 3 may have so much difficulty directing its energy that it becomes depressed because of its ineffectiveness at completing something. So many ideas, so little time.

The 3 also can talk itself out of virtually anything and become distracted or bored. Finding the tiniest fault with its big idea can stop it from proceeding past the fun part of invention to the part of implementation that requires diligence and persistence. The 3 loves immediacy. Although the 3 has a considerable amount of reserve and tenacity, it often spends its focus on other people rather than on itself.

As a result, the 3 can be a consummate procrastinator.

THE GIVER

The 3 is passionate, energetic, and fun. At heart, it is a giver and therefore must be careful about attracting takers. The 3 must learn to establish firm emotional boundaries given that its emotional state is more permeable than most people's.

The 3 craves relationships that stem from a deep emotional connection. It both wants and needs a partner who is emotionally available.

One of the most fundamental needs of the 3 is to be heard. It needs to engage with those who will encourage it to express its feelings and will consistently listen and support the 3 as it goes through its process of analyzing and responding to them.

The 3 must remember to take responsibility for its emotional expression in its relationships. To discipline itself so that it doesn't drown its significant other in its emotional life. There's a fine line between speaking the truth and sharing and "vomiting" out unprocessed thoughts and feelings.

The 3 is a natural counselor who sees potential in others, so it's drawn to form relationships with partners and friends who can be more like patients than equals. Either consciously or unconsciously, it thinks it can save or fix these people.

The 3 may also find relationships—overall—too confining for its passionate spirit. Sometimes a 3 wants to be married to its creative projects rather than to another person.

Alternately, the 3 could give up its independence in relationships and find its creativity squelched. It may dumb down its ideas so substantially to remain connected to a partner or friends that it feels it isn't living up to its ultimate purpose, which is when depression can become a regular force for the 3.

GET ON WITH THE SHOW

It's not surprising to find many 3s working in the fields of entertainment, politics, speaking, broadcasting, writing, and other industries that require expert communication skills, strong intellect, adaptability, and a good sense of humor. Any profession where someone can present ideas to an audience is right up its alley. But the 3 doesn't necessarily work well under the supervision of others or within a rigid structure. Interestingly, the 3 is the ultimate upcycler, or creative reuser. It learns about and experiences many different things and then takes everything it's good at and loves and puts it together to create something new and relevant for the world. The output of the upcycling can be an idea, a product, or a service—or just a way of viewing and engaging with the world. When the 3 is on a mission, it's in its element.

Remember, at the end of the day the 3 will inspire and uplift both itself and others.

A 3 often earns various degrees and certifications. If not trained in a formal way, its life experience makes up for the absence of education. The 3 often pursues many career paths or starts several businesses. A 3's life can read like a nail-biting, page-turning novel. Never a dull moment!

I've worked with many 3 Life Paths who personify the vibrant and engaging elements of the communicative and witty number 3. Often these folks have run the gamut with jobs, careers, and trainings and as they mature, find their way into an enterprise that uses many of the strengths and knowledge gleaned through their disparate experiences. I've known 3's who started as actors, got married and became a stay-at-home parent, went to grad school, worked as freelance writers, trained with some esoteric studies, earned certifications in a variety of things and then ricocheted into some other field of work (managing a grocery store, becoming a real estate broker, starting their own business in personal coaching). Yet at the end of the day, the common denominator is a positive outlook and a strong desire to help others.

THE FLIPSIDE OF NUMBER 3

CHAPTER 23

"I CAN'T DO THAT"

One of most significant obstacles to the full manifestation of the creative and intellectual brilliance of the 3 is intense self-doubt. Feelings of insecurity can stop the 3 in its tracks and stun it into submission. Fear of criticism hits a 3 very hard; so much so, in fact, that the 3 will often abandon or sublimate its original route because of having an unsupportive experience. Not to mention getting stuck in analyzing or overthinking every single thing it does. The 3 will mud wrestle with analysis paralysis repeatedly.

Especially early on in its life or career, the fear of criticism is stultifying. I once had a participant in a workshop who was a 3 Life Path. She shared a story about how she came from a family who was terribly abusive. All she ever wanted was to become a film editor. She applied to train as an editor at a school known for their exceptional media program and was set on leaving her abusive family dynamics and striking out on her own. When she was not accepted into the film program, she abandoned her dream of being a film editor. She never applied anywhere else or made any efforts to talk to anyone at the school about other options. She remained living at home and got a job at a coffee shop. One day she woke up with Bell's palsy, a condition that is often temporary and yet is the paralysis of one side of the face, which makes it very difficult to speak.

One of the lessons of the 3 is to cultivate the ability to apply itself. It needs to develop staying power, to trust its passion and strength, and then to do whatever it takes to gain expertise in the arena to which it is drawn. When the 3 experiences criticism or overwhelm, the best action for it is to *act*, even when feeling paralyzed—sometimes a small action is all that's necessary to shift out of paralysis. The challenge of the 3 is to buckle down and immerse itself so that it becomes a skilled practitioner as opposed to a dabbler who can't commit to anything other than a superficial knowledge of the task or skill at hand. If there's anyone who is easily distracted by "bright and shiny objects," it's the 3.

Interestingly, there is a meaningful nuance to observe regarding this advice. The delicate balance the 3 must maintain is in wholeheartedly pursuing its interests and buckling down to become an expert. The 3 is meant to do a variety of things and do them well. It needs to learn to juggle gaining knowledge and multiple skills; and to know how to differentiate this from just flitting from thing to thing.

RIDING THE WAVE RATHER THAN DROWNING

Number 3s make the "best" manic-depressives on account of experiencing extreme emotional highs and lows. Do not mistake this remark for criticism—or a true clinical psychological diagnosis—as this is merely an observation. Throughout its life, the 3 is learning how to experience and express emotion without getting stuck in negativity. If it's not using its talents or connecting with itself authentically, it will undergo intense mood swings. As a result, it needs to cultivate a habit, such as meditation, which can help it learn to ride the waves without going under.

I don't know a 3 Life Path who hasn't experienced some level of depression in its life. Often the 3 can go from feeling awesome to despairing in a moment (and back again), although this doesn't have to be a constant in its life. When 3s learn to identify when they are literally and energetically *depressing* their own emotions, creativity, and authenticity—then they can pass over into uncorking and elevating their true and joyful number 3 energy. The flipside of the 3 comes into play when it holds down, or suppresses, its natural emotions and creative impulses. The result is often a lingering depression that begins to define it.

Many numerologists call the energy of the 3 the *pleasant path*. Still I don't know any 3s who haven't endured substantial emotional trauma in their lives. The job of the 3 is to blaze through its own pain, find joy and optimism, and then model this behavior for others. Otherwise, the 3 can become a negative vortex who drags others down—the depressive cynic or person who lives superficially and detached with little to no contact with his or her authentic feelings. The 3 may experience a level of melancholy that lingers just underneath the surface.

"BUT IT LOOKS GOOD"

When a 3 is off track, one of its default modes is superficiality. The 3 can skim the surface everywhere it goes, stirring up emotional drama and trauma, feeling victimized, and placing all its energy into the shallowest elements of life. It can become slightly obsessed with appearance, focusing on its own wardrobe, beauty products and procedures, and those of others to the point of obsession

The 3 can be extremely impressionable. While this is part of its charm—enthusiasm, curiosity, and openness—it can also become problematic when not held in check. The 3 is the person you know who is always testing the new diet, taking the new supplement, buying the latest whatever-it-is, or ordering a piece of equipment they saw on an infomercial. While this isn't innately bad, the 3 can be so impressionable that it focuses the lion's share of its energy and resources on these sorts of things, much to the detriment of its overall success or satisfaction.

Another default of the 3 is to gossip. There are three levels of communication. The highest form of communication revolves around ideas and solving problems. The second form of communication revolves around the discussion of events. And the lowest form of communication revolves around talking about other people. The 3 can resort to the lowest form of communication as a means of diverting it from digging deeper within.

UNDISCIPLINED EMOTIONS

When the 3 wants the support of others to wallow in its own despair (which is a destructive form of emotional expression) it can cause its relationships to disintegrate. It desires comfort yet tries to make others into emotional garbage pails. In this scenario, the 3 is unwilling to work on finding positive solutions. It expects others to listen and verify every fragment of its intense emotional rollercoaster ride. And it doesn't realize that it has poor boundaries. It mistakes whines and complaints for intimacy.

The 3 also can procrastinate when feeling stuck or overwhelmed.

It even has a tendency not to let go of past relationships, mulling over them in its mind again and again, picking apart things said and done, what could've been, and what wasn't done, and so on. The 3 levels blame on itself and on others, tending to obsess over the smallest emotional hooks that bog it down with cynicism and emotional defeat. It will grind on an issue, shredding it until it turns into a pile of goo on the floor (so to speak).

When this transpires, if you are a 3, the best solution is just to leave things alone. Just stop mulling and grinding. If your input is vital and necessary, approach the issue freshly later when you are feeling less emotionally charged. Relationships can falter if depression becomes part of the daily existence of the 3.

THE GLASS IS HALF EMPTY

When off target, the optimistic and joyful number 3 becomes the anti-3. Instead of finding joy, it finds despair. Instead of engaging life with optimism, it's the ultimate pessimist. Instead of seeking fun, it judges everything and everyone as stupid. When a 3 is way off, the glass isn't just half empty, it's as if the waiter never came to the table with the water glass to begin with, and the 3 thinks it is everyone else's fault that the waiter ignored the table. A 3 who presents in this manner hasn't been able to muster the courage or resolve to move through emotional blockages and extreme self-doubt.

Honestly, there's nothing more grating than a 3 who refuses to embrace its birthright as a joyful, supportive, and emotionally communicative individual.

Often the off-track 3 is the guy or gal who talks all the time while saying nothing at all. I once knew a 3 Life Path who was a salesman and I would always walk away from our verbal engagements thinking: "I just spend two hours with this guy and he said virtually nothing that mattered!" It was all drama and recounting of who said what and how no one else was doing their job right. He was the one who would always make others bristle because he'd make off-color remarks, tell sexually explicit jokes, and generally behave in inappropriate ways. He had no ability to read social cues or to understand the ways in which he crossed personal and professional boundaries on a consistent basis.

CHAPTER 24

NUMBER6

6

NURTURER — VISIONARY — IDEALIST

AT ITS BEST

A 6's optimal expression is nurturing others while allowing them to lead their own lives without judging and criticizing them. The 6 energy allows for personal imperfection. This individual is a visionary who trusts and is inspired by its vision of the big picture.

The mission of the number 6 is to develop insight and acceptance in every aspect of life. Its purpose is to reconcile high ideals with practical reality and to accept itself, the world, and the present moment by embracing the perfection of all the apparent imperfection it encounters. The 6 is the vibe of home, family, love, duty, and service.

"LET ME DO THAT FOR YOU"

Overall, the 6 is known as the cosmic parent because its nurturing presence is felt everywhere it shows up. Understand that its primary task is to *modulate and balance its sense of responsibility*. Meaning, being neither overly responsible nor irresponsible. The balance imbued by the 6 energy is a lesson to be mastered whenever the 6 makes an appearance. It learns from the get-go how to take responsibility for itself, and then for others on top of that. As it matures, it attracts people and situations that require it to be the most responsible party. If the 6 shuns being the "responsible one," it leads a life of frustration and resentment.

The trick for the 6 is to learn to derive ultimate satisfaction from the responsibilities it agrees to take on—and not to allow itself to be held responsible when it feels used and abused.

HOME IS WHERE THE HEART IS

As a natural nurturer, the 6 leans toward combining love and marriage, like the proverbial horse and carriage. If it chooses not to be a parent, it parents in other ways, such as caring for pets, coworkers, and friends. There's a distinct, nurturing quality to the 6 that's coupled with a heightened sense of responsibility. The number even looks like it has a pregnant belly! It's pregnant with love and nurturing. As a 6, the individual is compelled to learn all about the domestic realm where home and family is a primary focus.

The 6 is "marriage and divorce" energy. As it's always working on perfecting the art of relationship, it often seeks an intimate one-on-one partnership and the security of home. It craves a happy, serene, and beautiful nest as a home base. Like the number 2, it seeks partnership and feels more complete and on purpose when in a relationship and when involved in positively serving family dynamics.

LOVE IS ALL YOU NEED

The 6 is devoted to service. It feels a sense of duty to family, country, or religion. Duty is just something that's an innate pull and a core value for this person. It is also a shining star with magnetism galore. People are drawn to the 6 and rely on its sage advice and example. It's a natural teacher and counselor and has an intuitive sense of people. It can see the whole picture in ways that most people can't. For this reason, it's more than happy to give advice to others—to provide answers, solve problems, and explain shortcuts. The issue for the 6 is this: Does anyone ever take its advice? Heck no! —or at least, less often than it would like

People only learn lessons by experience—not by being told what to do or to stop doing, or what to avoid. Experience isn't the best teacher, it's the *only* teacher. The 6 is consistently being asked to chime in or to get involved in other people's dramas, issues, and conflicts. It therefore can lean toward meddling and control rather than toward offering advice without an attachment to the outcome. The 6 emanates compassion. It loves helping and supporting others. But it tends to sacrifice too much in the name of love, duty, and service.

Ultimately the lesson of the 6 is to care for and nurture *itself* as much as it cares for and nurtures *others*.

"I CAN SEE CLEARLY NOW"

The 6 is highly creative and sees the world in an ideal sense, so it can get derailed or become easily frustrated if the world doesn't meet its high expectations. The internal dialogue is this: *Why can't everyone just see it can work this way?* And of course, when no one can see it, the 6 would love to throttle them until they do—because everything would be so much easier and better if they could just get it. The 6 sees solutions where people don't even see there's a problem and it can envision grandeur where others can't even see anything existing at all.

The key to success for the 6 is to understand that it needs to adjust its course early and often. It has the most success when it can troubleshoot and see the point of view of others. Even when it doesn't agree with another point of view, the 6 benefits from loosening its level of perfection and allowing more flow to happen, whether that's in a family dynamic or a work-related dynamic. The 6's visionary gift has the potential to make the world a better place on both the microcosmic and the macrocosmic levels.

IT'S A BEAUTIFUL WORLD

Intrinsically, the 6 is an artist and must find ways to use its creativity constructively. Otherwise, it defaults to frustration, which usually comes out as overinvolvement in the lives of those in its intimate circle and workplace.

The 6 has a natural propensity to cultivate harmonious environments. The beauty and balance of its domicile are imperative. It has an appreciation of texture, color, and placement, and the aesthetic richness that good design brings to the world. In fact, the 6 feels a sense of agitation if it finds itself having to deal with people or places it finds ugly or out of sync.

In terms of clothing and appearance, the 6 often displays a sense of style. How it looks physically is important to it. Similarly, the appearance of others holds weight with the 6 and makes a difference in its overall satisfaction.

YOU AND ME, ME AND YOU

While the natural habitat of the 6 is marriage and parenthood, also know that not every 6 chooses to marry. Sometimes a 6 ends up doing few go-arounds in the marriage department before settling on a permanent relationship. That's because of having lofty expectations about the nature of a partnership and family life.

The 6 feels most "at home" when literally at *home*. If happily married, a 6 would rather spend time with its spouse/life partner than with others. If single, it'll establish family dynamics in another domain, such as its workplace or in a spiritual community.

The 6 tends to throw itself into the lives of its children and can have difficulty seeing them as grownups once they reach maturity. Women with 6 in their charts tend to attract Peter Pans, men who have failed to grow up psychologically. Men with 6 in their charts tend to attract damsels in distress—women who act helpless, like little girls. In both cases, the 6s end up wondering why they're again the responsible party in a relationship. So, if you've got a 6 in your chart, be mindful that you'll be more fulfilled and joyful if you're partnering with an equal.

Domestic tranquility is the goal for the 6. It tends to put people—particularly its significant other—on a pedestal and then feels betrayed or disappointed when it discovers that they're only human. In the optimal, the 6 is the cosmic parent whose ultimate satisfaction comes from engaging in everything it does with nurturance, compassion, and love, and from allowing people to flourish in their own ways while it cheers on their efforts.

"DON'T TELL ME WHAT TO DO"

The 6 thrives when it has control over its destiny. It prefers to manage or own a business since it finds it hard to work for others and has trouble taking advice or instruction. If the enterprise it starts is a home-based business, all the better! The 6 is a natural with any profession where it can create something, sell it (or offer a service), and be its own boss. Anything having to do with healing or counseling is right up the alley for the energy of the 6, especially if it has to do with children, the elderly, family, or relationships.

Money flows effortlessly to the vibe of the 6 when it's engaged in something it feels is a service to others. Success comes easily when it tames its perfectionist streak and puts the focus on its creative and visionary goals. When centered on giving, service, and creativity, money also flows to the 6 almost effortlessly.

Often the 6 is highly innovative in the arts, particularly in the field of music. Sixes often sing and play instruments. Any career having to do with creating beautiful things is in line with this energy, including jobs in the beauty industry (doing hair and makeup), the clothing industry, interior design, or the art world. The 6 excels in justice-related fields, including police work, the law, and the court system. Sixes also make good firefighters and missionaries.

THE FLIPSIDE OF NUMBER 6

CHAPTER 25

PICTURE PERFECT

With the 6, life is all about learning to appreciate the perfection of the imperfection of everyone and everything, including itself. The 6 is a control freak. It often sets the bar so high that it's impossible for most people to meet its expectations—despite the fact that the 6 assumes they *should* already know what they're doing wrong. *It's. So. Obvious.*

And let's be clear: The perfectionist tendencies of the 6 start with its expectations of *itself*. It expects to go to the moon and back every day and has a harsh inner critic when its unable to do so. Remember—part of the mission of the 6 is to learn how to give itself the love and nurturing that it provides to others. It's always seeking balance. Often it takes years for the 6 to comprehend how high its standards are and why it feels so agitated or anxious most of the time. You might say: *If the 6 ain't happy, ain't no one happy!*

The 6 can walk into a room and silently punish those who aren't pleasing it or are failing to meet its current standards. It's admirable that it's got it together and has established an astronomically high approval rating, yet it achieves more balance and satisfaction when it gives itself and others a break occasionally.

The 6 would do well to use the fourth agreement from don Miguel Ruiz's *The Four Agreements* as its mantra. "Always do your best." The continuing message of this agreement is that "your best" fluctuates and isn't constant. The best one day might be just being able to roll out of bed. The best another day might be showing up and accepting an Academy Award. For the 6, satisfaction comes from making the best effort it can on any given day.

MOVE ASIDE

When the 6 feels unappreciated, undervalued, or overwhelmed, it tends to blast everyone around it with self-righteousness. Remember, the 6 is an idealist and therefore wonders why everyone can't be, feel, think, and achieve at its own high level of perfection. When the 6 turns into Judgey McJudgerson, it's not operating at its highest and best. It can exert crushing blows of criticism and judgment on those around it to everyone's annoyance and resentment. Sadly, one of its greatest talents is its ability to make others feel guilty or unworthy.

The irony here is that deep down the 6 feels this way about itself and is its own worst critic.

When feeling down or agitated, the 6 can put up a wall that is cold and punishing. The 6 is an "if you want something done right you just have to do it yourself" kind of vibe. It wants to be indispensable and then resents being indispensable, even if it's the one who set up a dynamic that way. The bottom line is that the 6 is functioning optimally when it is capable of seeing the perfection of everyone and everything being at whatever juncture they're at with their process at the moment. When the 6 lets go of its "shoulds" and instead relies on its incredible senses of nurturing, compassion, and service, it'll be the most content.

UNDER COVER

A loss of identity is common for the 6. It tends to submerge itself fully in the lives of its family members. It's so busy nurturing them and making the house a home, making a point of knowing who's allergic to what and what everyone's favorite foods and TV shows are that it has no clue what its own preferences might be. It's always serving others, frequently at the expense of self-care. Often this comes to a crisis point. When it loses its identity, it struggles to answer important, foundational questions like: Who am I? What am I doing? What do I want? When is it my turn?

In an article entitled "How to Stop being a Martyr," life coach Martha Beck aptly describes the life of the 6. She advises: "If you're chronically over-extended, underappreciated, and very, very angry, there's a simple solution: Stop playing the martyr."[1] She also observes that "often martyrs create and rehearse their parts in a dysfunctional pattern of interaction called the Karpman drama triangle. . . [which] involves three possible roles: victim, rescuer, and persecutor,"[2] and explains that the solution is to set boundaries and tell the truth. Often the 6 unconsciously creates drama.

If you're a 6 and feel like you're living in a state of melodrama, remember this simple, almost cruel fact: We train people how to treat us. Healthy relationships can only be established in an environment of authenticity. You must learn to be true to yourself and to tell people what that means for you. For all of us, being authentic is an ongoing task—yet for a 6, the added weight here resides in working against an innate sense of responsibility, duty, and service that can lead you astray.

For instance, I once worked with a 6 Life Path. Let's call him Christopher. He lived in a rural area in California and married his high school sweetheart at the age of twenty. He had never had a job working for an employer since he started a business selling plants, fruit, and other farm produce from his family's property when he in his early teens. His small entrepreneurial enterprise turned into a full-blown business. He and his wife eventually had a child. Christopher is a good-looking guy and presents as intelligent and charming to his customers. Yet his extended family would give a different perspective.

Christopher's behaviors with his family teetered on abusive. He would get into verbal, and sometimes physical, altercations with certain family members. The language he used with his wife was condescending and contemptuous. He would complain in the privacy of his own home about his customers and held himself and his own ideology about how one should behave in life to be the golden standard to which everyone should aspire. He was the harshest toward his family members, particularly his parents who had divorced, much to his disapproval. His siblings were also under fire and could never measure up to what he considered to be his own superior performance.

Christopher had a lot to learn about how to adjust his expectations and how to refrain from being highly critical and judgmental.

BRINGING THE DOUBLE 63 INTO THE 6

CHAPTER 26

The Master number 33/6 brings the double 3 into partnership with 6. The combination of these two numbers in these proportions leads to the magic, beauty, and harrowing journey of the Master 33/6.

Here are five suggestions for introducing the 3 energy to the 6 energy so that they become fluid and powerful dance partners in your life.

HAPPY TALK

The 3 and the 6 are synergistic, as both contain the energy of creativity on various levels. The exciting part is that you have two parts 3 and one part 6—meaning, for you the communicative and joyful elements of the 33 will fuse with the overall energy of the nurturing and responsible 6 that you embody. On the other hand, the 33/6 is a bundle of energy in which disparate needs and underlying drivers may be in competition. This may be perplexing, if not confounding. For example, the 3's natural habitat isn't necessarily the domestic realm, whereas the pull of the 6 is always toward home. This will be an important factor in your happiness. Never forget to create home even if your personal configuration doesn't look like a traditional model.

Your creative outlets need to be met and taken seriously. In *The Life You Were Born to Live*, Dan Millman makes the point that "the double 3 means that *inner expression* needs to manifest before *outer expressiveness* can bloom."[1] Striking a balance between inner and outer expression will be a life-long challenge for you, if you are a 33/6, given your perfectionist nature and your innate struggle to embrace how the world actually is rather than how you would like it to be—or know it should be. Because of this, self-doubt and perfectionism are the biggest stumbling blocks for the 33/6.

In a commencement address at Barnard College, Meryl Streep made an observation about how she began to navigate the world when she was a teenager. She spoke about being in high school and wanting desperately to learn how to be appealing. "I worked on what actors call my 'interior adjustment.' I adjusted my natural temperament, which tends to be slightly bossy, a little opinionated, a little loud, full of pronouncements and high spirits—and I willfully cultivated softness, agreeableness, a breezy, natural sort of sweetness. Even a shyness, if you will, which was very effective on the boys."[2] In many ways, Streep sounds like she is making a summary of the complex nature of the 33/6 insofar as there is an underlying stridency that works best when it's acknowledged and honed—bossy, opinionated, and full of pronouncements and high spirits!

The challenge is to own your voice, your values, and your identity, without asking others for permission to express yourself or seeking (or demanding) their approval.

DO I HAVE TO DO EVERYTHING?

Yes, you tend to be the micromanaging master or mistress of your—or *the*—universe. One of the contradictory things the 6 does best is to take responsibility for everyone and everything and yet resent the fact that no one else pulls their weight. Just a reminder: *We train people how to treat us.* You must hear this message again and again, through the loudest volume setting on the dial. The hyperemotional sensitivity of the 33 merging with the caretaking propensities of the 6 has the potential to turn you into an emotional satellite dish that will attract everyone's issues for you to fix, modulate, figure out, and make "all better." The funny thing about this is that it takes a very long time for most 33/6s to understand how exacting they are in comparison to the rest of the world.

Seriously, it could take a while to get to the point where you can—if you choose to—take a step back and lessen the impossibly high standards to which you hold yourself and everyone else. Your help may often come across as somewhat patronizing because—let's face it—it *is* condescending to do something for someone else just because you think they aren't doing it the right way or aren't capable.

"I DON'T WANNA"

Dan Millman observes that the 33/6 is prone to "disillusion, disappointment, and general frustration when life doesn't meet their expectations. Because of this, they tend to express themselves in the negative, through complaining, criticizing, gossiping, judging, or name-calling," citing self-doubt and perfectionism as the two biggest hurdles to be overcome.[3] It's a rather high-level mission when you're working the 33/6.

In their book *Numerology*, Kay Lagerquist and Lisa Lenard suggest that the "33/6 was thought to be the highest Master number, signifying the highest human consciousness possible. Because of this, the number 33 has been given nearly divine status, and called the number of the avatar. This number is on the journey of discovering its powerful healing energy through an open heart and unconditional love. Through love and example, the 33/6 awakens others to its depth and understanding of how to make spiritual truths work in the material world."[4]

Going about your Christ-like mission on a day-to-day basis can make you weary, mainly since you feel the vastness of both the joy and the despair of the world in soul lifting and soul-crushing ways. Some say that the Master 33/6 is the most influential of the Master numbers and you can see why. This vibe up levels the inspiration of the 11 and the tenacity of the 22 to an even higher octave of service and *being.*

OVER THE TOP

It's a perpetual challenge not to go overboard with emotional anxiety when you're working with the integration of the 33 and the 6. Both carry high levels of creative, artistic, and dramatic energy. One of the consistent challenges is to learn how to contain your depth of emotion while not squelching it. Astrologer Henry Seltzer once made this statement, and it's accurate for you if you're a 33/6: "The savior in you brings out the victim in another."[5] There is a tendency to swing with the pendulum of responsibility, opting for either far too responsible or far too irresponsible. Either way, often there's little room for gray when it comes to your status and your stance on the responsibility realm.

Let's be honest. Some folks with the Master 33/6 struggle intensely with the opposing forces this energy and mission bring to the table. Often a 33/6 can become either fragile to the point of chronic anxiety, even mental illness, or obstinacy resulting in pushing social boundaries to the limit. Some possible celebrity examples include Charlie Sheen (born September 3, 1965), Lindsay Lohan (born July 2, 1986), and Ben Affleck (born August 15, 1972). All these people show either a 15/6 Life Path (when calculated using the month/day/year calculation) or a 33/6 (when calculated using the long method). From an outsider's perspective, we might simply view some of their behaviors as volatile and excessive.

YOUR OWN HARSHEST CRITIC

The path of the 33/6 is rife with high expectations and extreme emotional sensitivity, so much so that no one (not even you) knows how inflated your standards of thought and action are. Day by day, you're learning to absorb and embrace the inherent learning process that everyone is going through with the understanding that this is what life entails. It's not the presentation of a result—it's *movement*—a dance into all that we are becoming. The 33/6 is challenged with taming idealism while holding onto a vision, which is one of your unique gifts.

If you're a 33/6, the keys to success in this regard are to modulate your sense of responsibility (the key for the 6) and discipline your emotions (the key for the 3). You benefit from leveling your expectations while remaining positive and upbeat.

Dan Millman maintains that the 33/6 swings "from manic over-confidence to depressive doubt. Very competitive, they constantly judge and compare themselves to others to see how they're doing. If they don't feel like they're doing well enough, they may push themselves, strive for lofty goals, and reach for perfection. If they succumb to self-doubt, they may step out of the game, just get by, or drop out, disheartened and defeated, victim to the logic, 'If I don't try, then I can't really fail.'"[6]

Also understand that you can be on the path of the 33/6 without being famous or well known. Many people with 33/6's in their numerology chart are regular people, just like you and me. Yet they are often called upon to help, heal, and inspire others. I know a 33/6 Life Path who came to live in the U.S. from another country. She is devotedly religious, fun loving, and upbeat. She has many friends and offers support before people even know they need it. She's married to a man who has needed more than his share of caretaking and she has provided this with good grace and with an amazing amount of endurance. Her family is her life and her heart, and she offers love and support wherever she goes. You don't have to be Mother Teresa to engage in the heightened calling of the 33/6, as long as you infuse unconditional love and a certain sense of lightness and joy into your daily interactions, you're right on track.

THE CHALLENGES WITH THE MASTER

33/6

CHAPTER 27

"CAN I TALK TO MY LAWYER?"

One of the essential tendencies of the 6 is its heightened sense of needing control and its desire for perfection which present themselves as strident judgment. If you're a 33/6, your superlatively high standards lead you invariably and consistently to feel let down and disappointed by other people and the world at large. You can be challenged by constant exasperation and feeling as if you're beating your head against a wall because of the overall demands of family, responsibility, justice, service, and duty. Most of the time you're the one who rushes in to help and support, knowing what others need before even they know. This heightened sense of how life should be can feel daunting. It may feel that your responsibilities are never ending.

The most prominent gift you can give to yourself—and in effect, to others—is to rid your vocabulary of the word *should*. Your strict sense of fairness can become more like a prison cell for you as you obsess over the smallest and the largest infractions both in your personal life and in the world at large. You can hang on to the battle cry "It's not *fair!*" to the point of self-destruction or at least to the end of diminishing returns. A default mechanism of the 33/6 can be to try to lay low and play it small to hold some level of control over a smaller fiefdom. Yet this isn't going to allow you to realize your potential.

REALLY?

The 33/6 feels a sense of enormous responsibility. The immense burden felt can manifest as being responsible for an abusive alcoholic husband, a self-destructive child, or a political party, religion, or humanitarian cause. The 6 often doesn't even realize how much of the time it's shouldering responsibility. The trick to overcoming this issue is gaining the awareness that *this is an issue*. Often the 6 is unaware of how idealistic its views are. It has a lot to learn about allowing other people to walk their own walk, even if it is painful to watch them falter.

On the other extreme, a 33/6 may shun responsibility like the plague or misuse their power. Like all people embodying the energy of Master numbers, the pull toward the oppositional aspects of your calling will need to be dealt with as you engage the demands of being a 33/6. It's imperative to learn healthy detachment while also following your calling and responding to the needs of others.

CAN IT BE DONE YESTERDAY?

Like the Master numbers 11/2 and 22/4, the Master 33/6 comes with a sense of urgency and volatility. The 3 (doubled in 33) signifies that you're on a spiritual path to enlightened caregiving and loving service. Sure, there are opposing elements here: The 3 gives you heightened emotional acuity, creativity, joy, optimism, and a capacity for higher levels of communication. The 6 adds a home and family element to your vibe, as well as an overall urge to act like a super parent and nurturer. Yet it takes time to get a handle on this ability, to differentiate your emotions from those of others, and to express your feelings in a healthy manner. You often end up eating your feelings or using them as a weapon until you get the hang of it. You may have come into the world with such a broad sensitivity to others that you stray from solidly identifying with your feelings to such an extent that you lose yourself. Or you may be a belligerent rebel who pushes the envelope of convention to the point of self-destruction or self-harm. Your desire to alleviate the suffering of the world may be compelling, yet you need to recognize that you can't achieve this feat single-handedly.

DETOURS

While everyone can suffer from an addiction, having a Master number in your profile may exacerbate the tendency to go through specific periods of time where you opt to numb out. The nervous tension you feel may seem so disconcerting that you will try to dampen it or to control it. Often using substances (food, alcohol, drugs) is the route taken, until you discover that a lifestyle of consistent meditation, exercise, and other forms of self-care that assist your incredible spiritual potential are better ways to cope with stress and release tension.

Being in alignment with the 33/6 means being focused on giving and service on a grand scale. If you're not focused on selfless service, you're not in alignment with your ultimate goals. You'll wrestle with feeling overburdened because you'll tend to be emotionally raw, taking in the wounds of the world. Even so, do your best to stay on the path of helping and healing in whatever form you choose.

Because the demands of the 33/6 are quite challenging, you can veer off track reasonably easily, becoming the anti-6—self-absorbed, struggling with addictions, and unable to channel your masterful energies constructively. You could become a professional paranoid and break apart from self-destructive rage or fear. This can play like an episode of "The Rise and Fall and Rise of [fill in your name here]."

With a Master 33/6, you're at your best when you embrace and act upon an inspired vision. You're a natural nurturer with a powerful gift for healing on both a personal and a grand scale, which is no easy task. You therefore must keep your feet on the ground and see the world realistically. Try not to get fed up or feel disappointed when the world doesn't meet your expectations.

REPEATING NUMBER 3

When you see a repeated 3, metaphysicians believe it's a message from the Ascended Masters. It's a message to be creative and have fun, and pay attention to your physical body and how you're using your energy. The 3 sends a message that there is a "birth" coming into play in your life which can manifest on whatever level your working with—whether with the conception of a baby or the design of an idea.

REPEATING NUMBER 6

When you see a repeated 6, it is a powerful message of love and encouragement to face your fears, challenge your concerns, and adopt a more open, accepting attitude. Some suggest that this repeated number is an invitation to embrace the divine feminine in yourself and all things. It's an opening to be in the physical world, yet also be of the spiritual world.

PART FIVE

EXPLORING YOUR CYCLES

CHAPTER 28

EXPLORING YOUR CYCLES

While the main intention for this book resides in providing a pragmatic lens through which to view the Master numbers as they influence your personality profile and overall purpose in life, it's also useful to gain an understanding about how the Master numbers show up during certain cycles of time. Therefore, we'll now go over some of those basics. Understand that when you begin to get a good idea about the energy and purpose related to each of the Master numbers 11, 22, and 33, you can truly bridge that information and apply it to your understanding of cycles of time you experience throughout your life.

Although there are other cycles, bridges, planes, and transits in numerology, for our purposes in this book, we'll define and outline the following two cycles: Personal Years and Pinnacles. If you choose to delve deeper into your chart, you can learn to apply the same information when the Master numbers appear during other cycles of time as well.

WHAT HAPPENS WHEN A MASTER NUMBER SHOWS UP AS ONE OF YOUR CYCLES?

CHAPTER 29

Master numbers may show up in your personality profile and they can also show up as the number for one of your cycles—most commonly, the Personal Year cycle. As we explain these cycles in this chapter, begin to plug in the information you have already learned about the Master numbers whenever they appear.

PERSONAL YEAR CYCLE

In numerology, it's believed we go through nine-year cycles throughout our lives and if you know the basic characteristics of the numbers 1 through 9 you can use that information to be in alignment with the purpose of your year. We all feel a change in energy at the end of each year, don't we? We start shifting our focus, delving into new feelings, and often these thoughts and feelings surprise us because they're so very different than what we've been prioritizing during the current year. Numerologically speaking, this is inevitable and undeniable.

Knowing the number of your Personal Year and of the Personal Years of those in your intimate circle is a fantastic way to understand how to mindfully navigate and create your most successful outcomes. The information provides you with the optimal qualities of the energy of the year and alerts you to the year's inherent obstacles so that you can make the best possible decisions. If you know the "theme to your party," you can understand the energy you'll work with during the year.

Here's how to calculate the Personal Year number. For this calculation, you use only the month and day of your birth, *not* your birth year. To these, you add the number of the *current year*. You can find the Personal Year number that you experienced in the past by doing the same thing, only adding to the year you want to know about rather than the current year. Of course, you may also project ahead to see what the Personal Year influence will be in the coming years. Also note that some numerologists believe that the Personal Year runs from birthday to birthday. Many other numerologists, myself included, feel that it runs from January 1 through December 31 of each year. Additionally, I believe that the energy related to your Personal Year intensifies around your birthday, approximately two weeks before and two weeks after your birthday. I also have noticed that the energy of the Personal Year crescendos in September and then begins to merge into the energies of your next Personal Year through the months of October, November, and December.

Let's look at an example of how to calculate the Personal Year.

Birthdate: September 9

Let's say the current year is 2018. In this case, add like this:

$9 + 9 + 2 + 0 + 1 + 8 = 29$

$29 = 2 + 9 = 11$

In this example, you would be experiencing a Master 11/2 Personal Year.

THE MASTER 11/2 PERSONAL YEAR

CHAPTER 30

This cycle holds the foundational energy of a 2 Personal Year and yet adds a spark—or a flamethrower—of the Master number intensity to the mix. As with all Master numbers, it's beneficial to first look at the foundational energy of the single-digit number and then take into consideration what the double-digit Master number brings to the table.

When you have a 2 as a Personal Year number, you can be confident that it's a time to slow down and develop *patience*. After a three-year period of intensity and transformation (the Personal Years 8-9-1, which always precede a 2 year) this year you have a "hall pass" to slow down, breathe, and focus on others.

The previous three years have been a self-focused period full of weighty transitions and transformation. The 2 year is a chance for your emotions and relationships take the front seat. Last year was most likely highly active and career-driven. This is a year devoted to love in all its forms. The 2 Personal Year is a slow-moving time designed to test your trust in right timing and is schooling you in the development of patience. It's an "us" year as opposed to a "me" year.

During a 2 Personal Year cycle, the universe has your back, yet you'll often feel as though it's snoozing on the job. It'll feel like you're moving three steps forward and four steps backward at any given time. You could think of this as the "tar walking" year where you might feel as if even the most basic step forward takes far too much energy, time, and patience. Levels of frustration can feel heightened. The highest and best use of the 2 Personal Year resides in slowing down, relaxing (if you can), and focusing on your relationships.

In business, the 2 year supports networking. Rather than placing one phone call a month or sending a terse email response, you'll benefit from really getting active with cultivating and honing in on your tribe. Concentrate on cultivating deeper connections within your inner circle. Speak your truth gently yet firmly. It's a fabulous time for attracting "the one" or reestablishing your connection with your significant other. However, don't expect anything to transpire at a rapid pace.

You could decide to marry or up-level your intimate relationship during a 2 Personal Year. If you're single, often you'll find a soul-centered mate and enjoy the additional time spent focusing on really getting to know each other. It's a testing year regarding setting firm yet supple emotional boundaries with friends, colleagues, and family. You'll be called upon to resign from being used as a doormat if that is something you previously found yourself succumbing to in your daily life.

Intuition can soar in a 2 Personal Year when you place perimeters around uncontrolled or undisciplined emotions. Your sense of style, design, and artistry of all kinds is also heightened. Optimally, this is the time to open and soften your heart, trust in divine timing, and develop healthy and authentic relationships. Patience is your key theme, right alongside cooperation. If you're a Type A personality, the 2 Personal Year can feel quite challenging.

In addition to the core elements of the number 2, you have the added intensity related to the Master 11 energy offering you additional challenges, yet the potential benefits are enormous. Along with it being a slower, relationship-oriented, and emotional year, you'll have opportunities to learn profound spiritual lessons. These lessons can manifest in every way imaginable—from learning what to do when coping with a crisis to learning how to embrace massive success.

With an 11/2 Personal Year, you might not feel as though things are slower at all given you're working with the double 1 energy. Yet even if it's a hard-driving year, you'll still experience more than your share of halts, delays, and issues requiring a heightened level of patience. These delays create space for amazing spiritual insights and advancement in intuitive ability. The Master 11/2 is a high-voltage energy, so you can be sure that the 11/2 Personal Year will test you to stand up for yourself, take the lead in your life, and tangibly manifest results. The challenge is in bringing heaven and earth together in a productive way.

You're always going to face challenges related to the oppositional elements that Master numbers bring with them. In the case of the Master 11/2 Personal Year, you can feel anxious and edgy even though—numerologically speaking—the number 2 offers a slower pace and a chance to concentrate on relationships. Perhaps you're a Type-A personality and the hovering required this year is a no-go for you. If you continue to think it's business as usual and are unwilling to back off just a bit from pushing and advancing things via your agenda, then this year can feel like a real kick in the pants. Just when you think things are in order and going your way, most likely it disintegrates right before your eyes as you frantically attempt to put it all back together the way you want it to be.

If emotions are a bit foreign or uncomfortable to you, then this cycle can feel very confusing. Or alternately, if you're an emotional person by nature, you can get carried away inside the cacophony of emotions and have trouble maintaining balance or equilibrium. One of the tricks of the 11/2 Personal Year is to follow up with right action while also being acutely aware of when you need to back off or let something develop.

If you're an 11/2 Life Path, during an 11/2 Personal Year, the core issues you naturally wrangle with will come at you with galactic force. Whenever we experience a cycle of time that's the same as our Life Path number, it'll push you to turn your core "triggers" into "treasures" instead. You'll be required to get up close and personal with the core lessons inherent in the Life Path number in an even more immediate way.

With that in mind, you can integrate and apply information about the Master number 11/2 when it shows up as any cycle of time. If the cycle of time that's involved is longer than a year, think of it more along the lines of a course of study your soul enrolled in for a longer period. Apparently, the lessons you need to learn will be more sustained and will more directly affect other aspects of your development.

THE MASTER 22/4 PERSONAL YEAR

CHAPTER 31

Let's go through an example to see how a Master 22/4 Personal Year might show up.

Birthdate: September 2

Let's say the current year is 2018. In this case, add like this:

9 + 2 + 2 + 0 + 1 + 8 = 22

In this example, you would be experiencing a Master 22/4 Personal Year.

This holds the foundational energy of a 4 Personal Year and yet adds a spark—or a shooting star—of the Master number 22 intensity to the mix. As with all Master numbers, it's beneficial to first look at the foundational energy of the single-digit number and then take into consideration what the double-digit Master number brings to the table.

When you have a 4 as a Personal Year number, get ready to batten down the hatches and get serious about the future. It's time to slow down, steady your pace, and become more methodical about the goals you want to achieve. Chances are you have some projects in the works that need to be tended to and nurtured. This will be a more serious year than others, requiring hard work to set the foundation for whatever you're working on, be it job, relationships, health, or family.

Often the early months of a 4 Personal Year feel invigorating in the same way that committing to a deep cleaning of your house feels good. It's like the feeling of satisfaction you get when you clean out the closets and donate stuff you haven't used in years to your local Good Will. Perhaps you also decide to replace the carpet and update the bathroom. Then you see how great everything looks and feels and take another step and choose to reorganize the office and change the window coverings. Oh—and now that you've done that, you realize you need to get all your files into one place, color code them, and box them by year and category. It starts to get more involved the longer you work at it. Get the picture?

So, understand that often there's a burst of energy and enthusiasm at the beginning of a 4 Personal Year and yet as the year wears on, it can start to feel slightly arduous. Therefore, it's a good idea right from the get-go to set a slow and steady pace that will get you to the finish line with more of your sanity and good humor intact than sprinting out of the starting gate in a mad frenzy to get it all done over the first weekend.

Since the energy of 4 is all about foundations, sometimes you'll find yourself building a house or moving to a new home in a 4 Personal Year. Home and your sense of security can take the front seat. When you're experiencing a 4 cycle, you'll also be confronted by limitation in various forms. How does this show up for you? A 4 Personal Year can challenge you with health, family, and career issues having to do with limitation. What limitations are to be worked with and negotiated through? What barriers are you creating for yourself that aren't necessary?

This is a cycle that tempts you either to overwork or to under work. Optimally, you'll need to forgo happy hour and stay a little later at the office to finish up that big report or file, complete the last part of the chapter you're writing, or think through the way you want to systematize your next project. While working so diligently may feel a bit thankless at times, you'll reap the rewards and be gratified when you accomplish your goals step-by-step.

This is a year to pay special attention to your health. You'll have to consciously take time for self-care—plan it and prioritize it. A 4 cycle also tests you with some old family issues bubbling to the surface that need to be resolved or dealt with differently. All in all, you'll glean the most satisfaction from your 4 Personal Year when you take the time to focus on the longer-range trajectory for your life.

Try to systematize your life in whatever way will make it much more efficient in the years to come—whether that's by focusing on work, getting your house in order, reviving your health, or healing family issues.

In addition to the core elements of the number 4, the added intensity related to the Master 22 will offer you additional challenges, yet the potential benefits are enormous. As you know, 22 is the most powerful number in numerology. It serves as the "Master Builder" and requires significant vision, focus, and hard work. This Personal Year is quite intense and prods you to up the ante with your work and career goals. It often goes hand in hand with expanding your enterprises and thinking big. There are many challenges inherent in this energy, including devoting yourself to your work efforts at the expense of personal relationships.

When you experience a 22/4 personal year, understand that you're working with the foundational energy related to the number 4 and then with the double 2. You'll need a lot of patience, an ability to "play well with others," and a willingness to share the sandbox.

You're being called upon to step up your enterprises and expand, to take risks and think bigger. But know that this is just the nuts-and-bolts phase. This is a time designed for marked and advanced achievement, as long as you're working with an altruistic vision. If you're on task, your endeavors during a 22/4 cycle can have significant influence and impact—not only on your own life but also on the world at large. It takes a mature sense of practicality, tenacity, and a focus on the greater good to fully harness the power of the 22/4.

It's imperative that you take time for breaks and short vacations during this time or your health can deteriorate due to physical and emotional stress. There will be strict deadlines to meet and often there are contracts and other legalities that come into play. All your effort and abilities will be used and tested during a 22/4 cycle.

Often people are stoked as they get into the 22/4 Personal Year. They feel the tremendous sense of satisfaction and accomplishment that comes with getting things in order and clearly defining their goals. If you're already an organized and achievement-oriented personality, the 22/4 Personal Year can be the time where you learn to roar. Alternately, if organization, system building, and getting serious about your endeavors makes you either fall into a coma or want to drop everything and head out to the bars, then you'll feel a lot of grief because nothing is moving forward as you hoped and everything takes much more effort than you think it should. Even the simplest things turn into a massive cluster of chaos.

Also, know that your life can feel off kilter if you're traveling a lot or if there's a lot of activity going on—even if it's not hard labor. It's common to view "hard work" as a ball and chain that needs to be escaped. This is not necessarily so. By hustling in a 22/4 year, you can make great strides in setting up foundations for your life and business as it moves forward. How successful you feel depends on where you get the most bolstering. Is your job okay but your intimate relationship a mess? Perhaps you need to commit to an actual home or geographical location. Maybe you're in a place in your life where everything is up in the air. *The energy of the 22/4 will force you to bring it down to earth in a practical, no-nonsense way.* If you're a 22/4 Life Path in the midst of a 22/4 cycle, the core issues you wrangle with will come at you with galactic force.

Overall, when you're experiencing a Master 22/4 cycle of any kind—whether it's a Personal Year or a Pinnacle cycle—you can be assured that you're in a period of intense high-frequency energy. This period demands that you step up your game by mastering successful forms of organization, management, and meeting (and surpassing) goals and deadlines.

If you have a service-based purpose or a humanitarian focus, the 22/4 is a dominant force that galvanizes your efforts and helps you make your dreams a reality. However, you must focus on balance, relaxation, healthy habits, and stress reduction during a Master 22/4 cycle, as well as on concertedly making strides to manifest your goals.

THE MASTER 33/6 PERSONAL YEAR

CHAPTER 32

Let's go through an example to see how a Master 33/6 Personal Year number might show up.

Birthdate: November 11

Let's say the current year is 2018. In this case, add like this:

November = 11

11 = 11

2018 = 2 + 0 + 1 + 8 = 11

11 + 11 + 11 = 33

In this example, you would be experiencing a Master 33/6 Personal Year.

This holds the foundational energy of a 6 Personal Year and yet adds a spark—or a rocket launcher—of the Master number 33 intensity to the mix. As with all Master numbers, it's beneficial to first look at the foundational energy of the single-digit number and then take into consideration what the double-digit Master number brings to the table.

When you have a 6 as a Personal Year number, get ready to put the spotlight on the domestic realm. After your freewheeling 5 Personal Year last year, it's time to buckle up and put on your big boy or big girl pants. It's a year devoted to home, family, and responsibility—a time to regroup, nurture, and be nurtured. There will be heightened levels of family-based responsibility this year. This is a time where all relationships are highlighted and under review. It's a good year to get married or engaged if you've been hovering around that decision.

This is a perfect year to attract "the one" or to recommit and "grow" your current intimate relationship. It's also a time where you may seek a divorce, a breakup, or other relationship splits. This could be called the "marriage and divorce" year—and that can be seen both literally and metaphorically. It's all about evaluating the relationships in your life, starting with your relationship with *you*. This is the year where you'll finally feel that "click" in knowing if a separation is necessary or you can also have the clarity you've been waiting for and officially say "I Do." Either way, these decision-making moments will peak this year.

The energy of the number 6 tests your sense of idealism, particularly when it comes to relationships. Do you give too much of yourself to your kids, spouse, parents, boss, or friends? Or do you level judgment on those around you, impeding your—and their—happiness? It's time to investigate how you feel empowered or disempowered in your domestic life. Oftentimes this is a year where you'll be asked to take on some additional responsibilities with friends and family that may come in the form of a wedding, graduation, birth of a baby, military deployment, a loved one's health crisis, or any other family event. The trick is to participate in the way you want to participate. Take on the responsibility without resentment or over giving. Or decide to take on the responsibility if your tendency is to avoid it.

This is also a year where your home takes a front seat. Do you have a desire to move? Redesign the kitchen or bath? Revitalize the yard with a new landscaping design, water feature, or planter? This is the perfect time to beautify your home on any level. On the career front—it's a "make or break" time for business. Your theme song for the year: "Should I Stay or Should I Go?"

This year of responsibility and relationship evaluation can offer a heightened sense of purpose and "warm and fuzzy" satisfaction in your home, family, and relationship life. It's magnetic for business and finances, yet not at the expense of your overall family obligations. This is a time to evaluate how you love, want to be loved, and how you relate to others. And yet it depends on how willing you are to take a deeper look at yourself and how you engage in relationships. If you find yourself pointing the finger at everyone else, then this can be a frustrating year.

The energy of the 6 brings out levels of idealistic expectations about the world at large—and about yourself and others in your closer circle. If critical judgment is your default mode this year, then the year can go awry. You can experience serious bouts of miscommunication and misunderstandings with those you love, if not those in your professional life.

The 6 Personal Year can also feel off if you fall into the irresponsible route, shunning involvement in building intimacy in your relationships and not paying attention to your home life—especially if you have children or other home-based responsibilities. Feeling exasperated and whiney is the first clue that you're not in the groove of the 6 Personal Year. How many eyerolls will it take to step back and reevaluated your perceptions and your stance? It can also feel out of whack if you've got blinders on or are in denial about certain key relationships in your life and you're unwilling to step up to the plate, have some hard conversations, and commit to changing the dynamic. If you choose the "same-o same-o," the 6 Personal Year will hit you like a wave at high tide.

Remember, if you're a 6 Life Path during a 6 Personal Year, the core issues you wrangle with will come at you with galactic force. When you experience a Personal Year that is the same number as your Life Path number, chances are that you'll be offered a heightened level of triggers that key into some of your biggest challenges and push you to step into your life path purpose in an amplified way.

In addition to the core elements of the number 6, the added intensity related to the Master 33 offers you additional challenges, yet the potential benefits are enormous. As always, the Master number brings nervous tension and intensity around the importance of your endeavors. A Personal Year guided by the Master 33/6 challenges you to—as Michelle Obama once said—go high when others go low. You'll most likely be faced with experiences and opportunities to hone your levels of unconditional love.

During a 33/6 Personal Year you might find yourself being called to write, teach, perform, or train others so long as your subject matter has a spiritual message or altruistic mission. You can be met with the desire to serve others on a grander scale or delve more deeply into your spiritual practice. When aligned with a higher mission, the double 3s offer a rather majestic ability to communicate, bring joyful optimism, and an upbeat message to a wide audience—whether that's an actual audience watching you perform or whether it's the people you engage and interact with on a day-to-day basis.

The likelihood of experiencing a Master 33/6 Personal Year is limited, yet it does exist. If you're one of the lucky few to go through this cycle, you have supportive energy around all your helping and healing endeavors, yet it's also challenging you to call in your inner (and outer!) Zen master. Accepting the imperfections of the world and of other people is mandatory. Relishing in small acts of gratitude and kindness is a must. Exacting positive influence and change in larger circles is favored. A 33/6 Personal Year cycle is a time to develop and act upon deep levels of selfless service and is a time to expand your message through humor, joy, and healthy emotional expression.

THE PINNACLE CYCLE

CHAPTER 33

In numerology, we all go through four distinct periods of time called Pinnacles in a lifetime. Each Pinnacle is a time of personal development. The First Pinnacle effects your formative years. The Second Pinnacle is a time of blossoming. The Third Pinnacle denotes a productive time and the Fourth Pinnacle can be seen as the time for harvesting what you've sown through the years. The Pinnacles can be conceptualized as a degree program you signed up for. You will remain on a particular campus while you study the same subject for an extended period. To extend this metaphor, the four Pinnacles make up the chunks of coursework you've signed up for throughout the university of your life. They are a master plan compartmentalized into stages of development.

The number of each Pinnacle represents the energy and lessons that are emphasized during a period of several years. Understanding the elements presented to you during your Pinnacle cycles offers you invaluable information about the focus and lessons to be learned during certain spans of time and also provides a really great format for understanding why certain things happen during these periods of time.

CALCULATING YOUR PINNACLE NUMBERS

Of course, as with every other number in numerology, there are several ways numerologists calculate the Pinnacle cycles. I'm sharing the way I feel the Pinnacles are calculated and yet I'll illustrate another way, too, so you can make the decision yourself.

First, this is the basic formula for finding your four Pinnacles.

Just like the proper way of calculating your Life Path number (separately adding the month/day/year), you work with the Pinnacles in the same way.

First Pinnacle = Month of Birth + Day of Birth

Second Pinnacle = Day of Birth + Year of Birth

Third Pinnacle = First Pinnacle Number + Second Pinnacle Number

Fourth Pinnacle = Month of Birth + Year of Birth

Let's see how you could do it both ways and how the results aren't necessarily the same.

NOVEMBER 22, 1985

With the first way of calculation, you would do the math using:

November = 11

11 = 1 + 1 = 2

22 = 2 + 2 = 4

1985 = 1 + 9 + 8 + 5 = 23

2 + 3 = 5

Then you calculate this way:

First Pinnacle: (month) 2 + (day) 4 = 6
Second Pinnacle: (day) 4 + (year) 5 = 9
Third Pinnacle: (first Pinnacle) 6 + (second Pinnacle) 9 = 15
1 + 5 = 6
Fourth Pinnacle: (month) 2 + (year) 5 = 7

Now let's see the other option. In this way of thinking, you use the full number without reducing it first. And when you have a Master number, the Master number is never reduced.

November 22, 1985

November: 11

Day: 22

Year: 1985

First Pinnacle: (month) 11 + (day) 22 = 33

Since 33 is a Master number it is not reduced. This is the final number for the First Pinnacle.

Second Pinnacle: (day) 22 + (year) 1985 = 2,007

2 + 0 + 0 + 7 = 9

Third Pinnacle: (1st Pinnacle) 33 + (2nd Pinnacle) 9 = 42

4 + 2 = 6

Fourth Pinnacle: (month) 11 + (year) 1985 = 1,996

1 + 9 + 9 + 6 = 25

2 + 5 = 7

With the first way of calculating, the Pinnacles show as:

First Pinnacle: 6
Second Pinnacle: 9
Third Pinnacle: 6
Fourth Pinnacle: 7

With the second way of calculating, the Pinnacles show as:

First Pinnacle: 33
Second Pinnacle: 9
Third Pinnacle: 6
Fourth Pinnacle: 7

The biggest change with doing the calculation the first way or the second way is minimal when calculating Pinnacle Cycles and often reveals a Master number.

HOW TO CALCULATE YOUR AGE AT THE TIME OF YOUR FOUR PINNACLES

Now you must calculate the age you are during your different Pinnacles.

The age in which you begin and conclude each Pinnacle Cycle depends on your Life Path number.

To calculate your age during your First Pinnacle, take the *number 36* and *subtract* your Life Path number from it.

Example: If you are a 9 Life Path, subtract 9 from 36.

36 − 9 = 27

This means that your First Pinnacle transpires from the *time of your birth (0) until you're 27 years old.*

To calculate your age during your Second Pinnacle, *add* 9 to the ending age of your First Pinnacle.

Example: For the 9 Life Path whose First Pinnacle ended at age 27 we calculate: 27 + 9 = 36

Your Second Pinnacle, in this case, lasts from age 27 to age 36.

To calculate your age during your Third Pinnacle, add 9 to the ending age of your Second Pinnacle.

Example: For the 9 Life Path, whose Second Pinnacle ended at age 36, we calculate: 36 + 9 = 45

Your Third Pinnacle lasts from age 36 to age 45.

Your Fourth Pinnacle starts at the end of your Third Pinnacle. This age initiates the energy surrounding you for the rest of your life.

Example: For the 9 Life Path, whose Third Pinnacle lasted until age 45, the Fourth Pinnacle begins at age 45 and lasts until death.

MASTER 11, 22, AND 33 PINNACLES REFERENCE GUIDE

CHAPTER 34

11/2 PINNACLE

When this is your Pinnacle number, you're being beckoned to envelop yourself in the elements of learning to *cooperate, share, be considerate of others,* and *be at your best when you are in harmonious relationships without sacrificing yourself in the process.* The number 2 is the number of partnerships, patience, balance, and diplomacy.

Yet remember, with the presence of the double 1, the softer elements of the number 2 are challenged with the necessity to also integrate the more forceful and initiating energy of the 1. Therefore an 11/2 Pinnacle can be a time where a desire for love takes front seat, whether it's through marriage or partnership, parenting, or other experiences that have the elements of unconditional love at the core.

This is a time where you'll be called upon to work on—and perfect—your subtle art of relating. Yet this is also a spiritually illuminating time and so there's the rub! How to balance the disparate energy of the innovative and independent 1 with the diplomatic and peace loving 2? An 11/2 Pinnacle is earmarked for the development of intuition, creativity, and opening yourself to the mysteries of the universe. This energy asks you to pay attention to details and practice patience and tact. This is a time where being an integral part of a group or community is where you feel most satisfied, comfortable, and confident. It's also a time where you can experience intense experiences that open you to developing patience and yet it can also be a time for fame and stepping into the spotlight. The key will be to infuse a higher sense of service and love into whatever you do. It's a time to define who you are while not getting lost in self-absorption.

22/4 PINNACLE

A 22/4 Pinnacle is a period where you're being called to build your life with solid, stable foundations that'll last. This is a cycle earmarked for marked achievement and demands a slow and steady pace to build something of lasting value.

This isn't a particularly lighthearted time because you're learning and being tested by issues related to *hard work, organization, setting up effective systems, patience, endurance, working step-by-step,* and *moving ahead methodically.* This stage is for designing and pouring the proper foundation for your future. It's a practical time where you're putting your ideas into the material world and manifesting your vision with discipline, limitations, and a serious attitude.

Frankly, it's not a time to mess around. You're being immersed in the energies that support a practical and realistic approach to life. So, a demand for order, system building, and organization is key. The 22/4 Pinnacle encourages you to be dependable, conscientious, realistic, and reliable. Determined and somewhat relentless effort is required, and you may feel a strong compulsion and emotional need to immerse yourself in work during this Pinnacle. When you do, you'll thrive on that energy and feel satisfied with the tangible results you create. Projects created or advanced during a 22/4 cycle are meant for the long haul. This period of time is earmarked for substantial achievement.

33/6 PINNACLE

Love, duty, responsibility, service, and *family* are the hallmarks of any 33/6 Pinnacle. This is a stage in your life that's immersed in the energy of nurturing and the Master 33/6 extends this into a higher level of selfless service. You may choose to nurture your career or your family—or even your pets or employees—yet you can't avoid these years that are devoted to nurturing those around you, embracing your sense of responsibility, and balancing giving to others and giving to yourself simultaneously.

This is a time where *home* takes on new meaning. It can be the time where you focus on establishing and maintaining your "nest," whatever that specifically means to you. It's a prime time to either get married or settle in and appreciate your home life and your relationships. If your giving is lopsided and you give to everyone else and leave nothing for yourself, you'll certainly experience the difficult lessons that accompany that imbalance. Or if your behavior is lopsided in the opposite direction, where you're self-involved and self-absorbed at the expense of giving freely to others, you'll certainly experience the difficult lessons that accompany that imbalance. You must achieve balance within yourself and your chosen family.

This is the stage where you'll be called to teach, counsel, or otherwise engage with serving others. It's a cycle where you're meant to develop a heightened sense of spirituality and spiritual purpose. You can benefit financially during this Pinnacle when you are solidly focused on your visionary contributions and service. So long as your intentions are altruistic, this is a time to expand your reach with any kind of performance, teaching, or counseling, or any other avenue where your communication skills can be developed and perfected.

The core purpose of this cycle is to develop unconditional love on all levels. This is also most certainly the "love and marriage" stage with intense focus on children and the home. It can also be the "marriage and divorce" stage when the marriage as it stands can no longer be positively sustained. Depending on which Pinnacle Cycle (First, Second, Third, or Fourth), it can be earmarked for nurturing a family or for branching out and providing your nurturing energy to reach a wider audience.

PART SIX

MOVING TOWARD MASTERY

CHAPTER 35

OBSERVATIONS ON MASTER NUMBERS

"I was a seeker for a long time, but I'm not seeking anything anymore. I feel like I don't need anchors anymore, because there's no boat to anchor, and you only need anchors if you have a boat."[1]
—Jim Carrey

DUALITY AND POLARITY

While being human is a somewhat complicated enterprise, having one or more Master numbers influencing your dance with life adds layers of intensity to everything you do. I find the most important yet most challenging thing to understand and act upon is the contrasting and oppositional forces that are inherent to Master numbers.

Esther Hicks, the channel for Abraham, says it best in her lectures (and I'm paraphrasing here): "Beliefs are just thoughts you choose to think over and over again. If you change your thoughts, you change your beliefs."[2]

One of the thoughts you with Master number(s) will benefit from is exploring, with more intimacy and depth, the notion of duality. The principles of polarity and opposition. Some people refer to this as non-duality. *Non-duality* means "not two" or "one undivided without a second." Non-dualism is an evolved state of consciousness, in which the dichotomy of I/other is transcended, and awareness entails 'centerless' and 'without dichotomies.'"[3]

The idea that the coexistence and acceptance of what Abraham-Hicks deems *contrast* is something that's a core issue. Keeping in mind that the Master numbers are innately in conflict with themselves, can you learn how to hold opposed ideas/stances/viewpoints in mind until they form a stronger, more complete whole? This is rather like placing molecules of opposing elements in a Petrie dish and having them miraculously bind into a stronger, more resilient new substance. When working with a Master number, you're dealing with this strange alchemy every day. How can you be durable, yet soft? Practical, yet open to new ideas? Compassionate, yet acting with healthy emotional boundaries? Allowing and surrendering to a "higher power," yet taking steps to attain tangible goals?

With a Master calling, it's imperative that you learn how to embody duality, opposition, and polarity. While many people are walking contradictions, you're the poster child for the delicate balance of yin/yang, light/dark, expansion/contraction. Your engagement with the tension of managing contrast is heightened and never lets up. Life naturally feels like a pressure cooker to you. Numerology in your case offers important guidelines for optimizing your experiences by unequivocally pointing out the intricacies of your energy and purpose. The goal here is for this information to give you a respite from whacking yourself over the head with the sturdy object of your choice (a hammer, brick, a criticism, or whatever you metaphorically use on yourself) while guiding you to open up your viewfinder and usher you into your highest self and the fulfillment of your advanced purpose. The key comes when you replace the question "Why is this happening to me?" with "What is this trying to teach me?"

Keep in mind that you will have several "lifetimes" during this one life. Occasionally life will knock the wind out of you, knock you down, or knock you out for a while. Treat life like it is a marathon. Sprinting or rushing may cause burnout, injuries, and breakdowns.

Philosopher Alan Watts offered some wise words that may shift your perspective about how you judge yourself.

> The existence of the universe is fundamentally playful. There is no necessity for it whatsoever. It isn't going anywhere. It doesn't have a destination to which it ought to arrive. It's best understood by analogy to music. Because music, as an art form, is inherently playful. We say you play the piano. You don't work the piano. Why? Music differs from, say, travel. When you travel, you're trying to get somewhere. In music, one doesn't make the end of the composition the point of the composition. If that were so, the best conductors would be the ones who played the fastest. And there would be composers who only wrote finales . . . same way with dancing. You don't aim at a particular point in a room because that's where you will arrive. The whole point of the dancing is the dance.[4]

As someone with Master energy in your mix, the sense that you must get somewhere, that your purpose encompasses something substantial and important, is a kooky oxymoron. You are meant to excel and contribute. Your birthright is to balance, juggle, and embody contrasts in authentic and efficient ways—while also balancing, juggling, and integrating them in spiritual, and deeply personal ways.

Your purpose is significant, yet how will you determine the degree of that significance? You can achieve your Master status by instituting a successful business or surviving a harrowing accident. You can step into your power by creating art or by offering solace and love to people on an individual level. You can be a subtle force of nature or a tsunami. And you can be different things at different times in your life—a stay-at-home mother who is a wildly successful entrepreneur. An engineer turned spiritual healer. A recovered addict who becomes a best-selling author.

There are so many avenues through which to activate and use your Master frequency for your own benefit and to benefit others. Often, activation is merely a matter of permitting yourself to do what your heart calls you to do without listening to the outer static in your environment or falling prey to inner chaos. The real kicker is that *the not knowing* of the Master number is part of *the ultimate knowing.*

I'm not trying to sound like Yoda here, yet think about it. When we question, search, and then finally feel we're at rock bottom—stuck, at an immovable impasse, facing the dissolution of everything we think we know and count on to define our existence in the world—this is when the rubber meets the road. When we're crushed or have to draw upon our inner resources, this is when we learn about ourselves, who we are, and how resilient we can be. Ask anyone who is successful, and they will tell you how they bounced from this job to that, or from an ill-advised relationship to something else. How they were ruined financially, probably more than once. How they failed and failed and failed again—and where they find themselves now has virtually no bearing on where they thought they'd be. I don't know how many times I hear this: "This can't be my life! This is not where I thought I'd be at this point!" Do you know anyone who—if asked ten years ago—is doing what they imagined they'd be doing?

A crucial shift in perspective—especially valuable for those with Master numbers in their charts—is to come to terms with the notion that *you are where you are supposed to be*, which doesn't mean that you just sit around and cave into indecision and inaction. It says that you're able to embrace levels of development and critical experiences from an enlightened perspective. If you find yourself in despair, remember that you have the tools to readjust, reinvent, and move forward while experiencing and integrating the powerful emotions that come with these vast transformations.

HARDSHIP

Having a Master number in your chart intensifies the lessons you can learn from life's difficulties. You'll go through various levels of response, depending on the severity of the problems you experience. Sometimes we're the ones creating our hardship by not trusting our gifts and failing to devote ourselves to doing what we know to be our true purpose in life. Many folks with Master numbers are expert at making mountains out of molehills while others experience genuinely great hardships.

Since you're working with the constant push of the Master number, you're always in a hurry to "get there," which can also feel hard. You'll confront substantial challenges in *getting there*, and often find yourself wallowing in places that you probably could have hydroplaned over. This is commonly the case in emotionally based situations. Remember the overall infusion of the sensitive number 2? Often having a Master number places additional emotional strain on you that can hold you back. This is the reason why a gift you should give yourself as early as possible is emotional self-discipline. Learning to embrace and use your natural intuitive skills is also an integral part of a Master path.

There are many ways to learn emotional discipline: energy work, therapy, and meditation are just a few choices. Being disciplined doesn't mean blocking or denying your emotions. It means modulating them and seeing them for what they really are: messages. For instance, I've known 22/4s whose life story centers on the *limitations others have placed on them*. This becomes the fabric of their lives and the foundation for their ongoing frustration and lack of achievement. For instance, they can feel that their parents didn't support them or love them adequately and so unconsciously they chose partners who are abusive or who they must take the lion's share of care for and can't move past it. They feel done-in and tired and carry that "put upon" energy with them into all their engagements.

The key to functioning well with a Master number is to be able to pinpoint, with the power of numerology, where your core issues reside and then dismantle them. Meaning: If you can see that no one is *making* you do anything—that you, in fact, are the only one making yourself do something—then this moment of awareness is when you can disrupt the cycle. When you can see you're in charge of your destiny and have a strong desire to change a negative pattern, that's when the magic happens.

This doesn't mean that the second you decide to change something it all runs smoothly, is all done, or is comfortable. Oh, no. It takes repetition to practice this skill, and you'll experience the intense recurrence within the themes your numbers bring with them.

DEPTH OF THOUGHT AND ACTION

Let's face it. You experience everything on a profoundly deep level. Sometimes it might take a while to step into this depth, so you might spend some years treading through "superficial land." At the core, you can't tolerate the static and drama that come from interacting with people who aren't interested in self-actualization or spiritual evolution. One of the issues you are likely to face, though, is that sometimes you just need to lighten up.

Seriously, just be human for a moment. It will often be through connecting with others that some of your greatest ideas come to fruition. When you're operating with a Master vibe, you'll experience inexplicable depths of both ecstasy and frustration with life. Sometimes you embrace this and roll with it, and sometimes the despair can overtake you. You're learning to move through all of it with a certain level of grace, resolve, tenacity, and flow. It's a practice sport that requires your participation all your life.

There are times in the Master trajectory when it feels impossible to achieve a level of satisfaction and contentment commonly labeled "happiness." Those with Master numbers feel an innate sense of volatility and edginess that lead them to seek refuge from the confines of the material world at different times during their lives. With a Master mission, the problem is that you care *so much* that the best way to survive is to *stop caring*. Strangely, when you end your attachment to outcomes, you recalibrate yourself and become more centered and intuitive. This creates a profound sense of flow. When you stop caring and start flowing in this way, the magnitude of your Master power unleashes. This doesn't mean you stop caring. It means that you stop caring in the non-productive or frustrating way that you're accustomed to expressing concern. It means to support the best way you can without taking on the full responsibility of the outcome.

By not caring in this old way you disengage from anxiety and projecting certain results and instead actually allow yourself to *embody yourself* in a way that was blocked by incessant projection, anxiousness, and fear. To quote Tony Robbins: "Joy is very easy to feel when fear is no longer dominating your soul. And sadness is fear that you've hung on to for too long."[5]

EGO AND HUMILITY

We've spoken of this before, and yet it merits being highlighted again. With great power comes great responsibility. As you blaze your way forward on your Master path, you'll need confidence to execute your responsibilities. You need a healthy ego. During one of his three-hour stand-up shows, co-median Eddie Izzard once observed that it takes a certain amount of ego to step out onto a stage by yourself in front of thousands of people and think you have something to say that is worth hearing. I agree. A level of self-worth must be in place if we are to do great things.

There's a "sliding scale" in the range between having a self-serving ego and an appropriately strong sense of self. Your success is a matter of formulating a strong enough sense of identity to help you achieve your destiny to lead, love, create, and achieve. Often those with Master numbers struggle with stepping into their power on a consistent basis and volley between feeling self-important and feeling unworthy or insignificant.

STRUGGLE INTO ENLIGHTENMENT

I don't know anyone with Master numbers who hasn't run the gauntlet as they experience the intense struggles that lead them, ultimately, into enlightenment. Or into their higher evolution or spiritual calling—or the quagmire of whatever the flipside of their calling might be. Often those with Master numbers go through periods of time—either long or brief—when there are high levels of procrastination or of feeling very stuck and undirected.

To quote Adyashanti: "Enlightenment is a destructive process. It has nothing to do with becoming better or being happier. Enlightenment is the crumbling away of untruth. It's seeing through the facade of pretense. It's the complete eradication of everything we imagined to be true."[6] If this notion is taken to heart, certainly happiness is not the end goal for the initiate with Master numbers. Instead the Master lifetime is bringing you into a more evolved level of contentment, flow, and universal understanding and wisdom.

Many numerologists have observed that Master numbers can be found in the charts of folks who are homeless, in prison, and facing other circumstances that we might not consider positive or in alignment with the higher demands of the Master 11/2, 22/4, or 33/6. The calling of the Master numbers is a huge leap from the abyss—meaning, if you're often faced with extreme circumstances you must find avenues where you can navigate and contribute to the betterment of yourself and the world at large based on your inherent purpose and gifts.

Those with Master numbers often sublimate their needs, desires, and ambitions to those of others—or the opposite: They allow their needs, desires, and aspirations to run away with them. It's a challenge to honor their higher calling while bringing themselves down to earth.

Master numbers are innately disruptive—they cause us to push, reveal, question, dream, and visualize. *Ultimately your job, if you possess Master numbers in your chart, is to step into yourself while also getting over yourself.* Yes, you signed on for overtime. Yes, you signed up for the accelerated program. You are indeed meant to leave a lasting impression in this world.

COMPELLING

People with Master numbers have a special something that others can sense. This can come across as magnetism or an energy that people find either mysteriously attractive or intimidating. Or both! Think about some well-known people with Master numbers—Tony Robbins, Ronan Farrow, Leonardo DiCaprio, Jerry Seinfeld, Oprah Winfrey, Matthew McConaughey—just to name a few. Master numbers aren't limited to celebrities. There are plenty of "regular" people who carry a Master vibe—and if you're reading this you're probably one of them!

LOTS OF INTENSITY

Intensity is the name of the game with these folks! Something is compelling about them, and this extends to everyone whose chart holds one or more Master numbers. If that is you, your magnetism will depend on how aligned you are with the expansive energy the Master numbers demand of you. You have an absolute advantage from the get-go because you bring a level of intrigue to the game of attraction. People tend to be fascinated by you.

CUT YOURSELF SOME SLACK

Those with Master vibes push themselves to the limit without realizing they've gone there until there's a meltdown, a breakdown, or an unraveling. Reaching the limit can show up in both subtle and dramatic ways.

One of the more significant lessons to be learned as you carry forward with your specific Master plan is that you can (and must) occasionally permit yourself to chill out for a moment. Sometimes you just need a break.

Some people decide to focus on raising their children at the expense or downplaying of their careers, and then they pick up the reins and blaze forward with their jobs when the kids are older and more independent—as opposed to trying to do it all at the same time. That's a kind of "resting" too. Oprah Winfrey once was asked if she thought you could have it all and she replied: "Yes, you can have it all. Just not all at once."[7] While I agree with this remark on a broad theoretical level, I also ultimately disagree. And here's my rationale. Oprah has said that she made a conscious choice not to have children because she knew that she was married to her career and having children would have put her in a position to be a not-so-great mom and always feel like she wasn't able to put her all into her enterprises. So, I would say that if Oprah truly wanted children, then her statement that you can have it all—just not all at one time—isn't true. She made a conscious choice to forgo children and traditional marriage to achieve her higher purpose.

I use this as an example because I run into people with Master numbers again and again who have an apparent conflict with similar issues. I have known people with Master numbers who kept their careers on hold while raising children and then launched them again after the kids reach adulthood. They said they felt the regret or frustration of prime career time lost that would never return, triggering the fear of always being behind. While this can be a common thread for people in general, those with Master callings feel this conflict even more severely.

Or alternately, some bypassed having a family and then had the wistful feeling that they missed out on an important part of life.

Whatever you choose to do to prevent overexertion and breakdowns, the reminder here is that you're a fantastic manifesting agent. If given clarity of focus, opportunity, and drive, there are choices to be made along the way.

DID YOU CHOOSE THIS?

If you believe in numerology, you likely also believe that we incarnate again and again and come into our physical bodies with individual soul contracts to fulfill. If you were born with Master numbers, you can be sure that you checked in with an elevated agenda and have some past-life wisdom and knowledge at your disposal. The key is in learning how to locate it and trust yourself even when you have no idea how you have access to certain feelings or certain information. Those with Master numbers benefit greatly by tapping into their own intuitive language. Do you see energy? Do you have precognitive dreams? Do you *just know* things? Do you notice messages through repeating numbers or other avenues of spirit communication? These are elements to make friends with and cultivate to make your Master mission more successful and more fun!

You might conceptualize yourself as a little soul spark out there, getting ready to incarnate again in whatever capacity. You feel all light, and clear, and you're somewhat full of yourself. You think, *Hey, this Master thing is right up my alley. Sign me up!* It's kind of like signing up to run a marathon when you're with a few friends who double-dare you or get you to sign up after you've had a few cocktails. You sign on the dotted line and then—*zip!* —you land on the density of Planet Earth. *Now what? What was I thinking?*

This would be the moment we find ourselves a bit shell-shocked, pumping our fists at the sky, and lamenting that we didn't know how tough this would be, so could we please cancel our contract?

Understand and remember that the Master numbers bring a higher spiritual function, no matter how you define that prospect. The Master numbers bring a higher vibration and a spiritual purpose for you to fulfill. Energetically speaking, they're always pushing those of us who possess them to a higher form of self-realization and self-actualization.

A Master number demands expansion and evolution, yet development and growth most often take place during—or in response to—severe or intensified circumstances. And yes, you did sign up for this plan. Even though you might curse it or wonder how you could have thought that it was anything even nearing a good idea, *you came in with all the tools to play out and succeed with your Master purpose.* Part of this purpose is finding your way to that purpose, defining it on some level, and then boldly forging ahead with your individual power and passion.

MASTER NUMBER SURVIVAL GUIDE

CHAPTER 36

PSYCHIC SELF-PROTECTION

Everyone working with Master numbers needs to learn methods of emotional and psychic self-protection. Knowledge and a basic understanding of energy anatomy are mandatory. You can feel drawn toward energy work or find yourself in dire circumstances that ultimately bring a level of "woo-woo" into your life. Often those with Master numbers experience and emotional or health crisis that forces them to seek help from alternative sources.

Understanding the chakras and how energy and energy healing operate is imperative. Especially necessary is energetic hygiene—cutting energetic cords and clearing yourself energetically every day. There are many ways to accomplish this kind of cleansing, and you will find your preference as you research it. The key is that whatever method you choose should be easy, repeatable, and efficient because this isn't going to be something you do just once and then return to business as usual. This needs to become a part of your daily routine.

MOVE YOUR BODY

Oh, I know. Everyone needs exercise. But you need more. When you're working with the highly intense Master energy, there's a lot of nervous tension and over thinking of things. If you don't exercise on a regular basis, it's like you're a bottle rocket that someone has lit and shoved into a can. All that explosive energy must go somewhere, and if you don't disperse it healthily through physical exertion, it will likely explode outside you or implode inside you. You need to sweat and to take time to strengthen and stretch your body so that it can sustain your high-powered spiritual journey. Exercise also serves the function of getting you "into your body." When you have the highly charged energy of a Master number, it's easy to become stuck either in the ethers or in your head, so much so that you can become accident prone and will be susceptible to weight gain and health concerns. You must prioritize physical exercise, good eating habits, and overall self-care. Keep it moving!

OM. OM. OM.

Meditation comes in all forms. With a Master number, you're called upon to step into a more evolved and spiritual life. Learning how to silence the mind and discipline your thoughts is imperative if you are to achieve the most focused and successful results—not to mention maintaining a certain level of sanity. Of course, one of the problems is that you don't think you have the time to waste sitting around doing nothing! Actress Cleo King (who happens to have a Master 11/2 Life Path) shared this on her social media page. I hope it inspires you to start or continue with whatever practice you choose. She said: "I used to say I don't have time for meditation. But now that its daily, *the calm!!*"

This is just one of the many counterintuitive issues you'll be faced with again and again. You'll be amazed how much more productive you can be if you engage in a consistent meditation practice. We're not talking about spending hours a day in a cave somewhere—unless you're up for that. Just work meditation into your daily life in whatever way serves you best. Can you give it ten minutes or an hour a day? Whatever you can commit to is excellent.

Your style of meditation could be a walk around a lake or in the woods. It can come into play during a jog or a yoga practice. You can meditate while you dig in the garden or take a swim. You can sit on your meditation pillow and do it that way. You know this works and it's more useful than medicine, even though it's most likely the last resort when you're feeling stressed or going through some turmoil. Whatever style works for you, do it regularly.

GO OUTSIDE!

You need contact with the natural world. You recharge your batteries when you take time in nature in whatever way speaks to you—hiking, gardening, or doing anything in or near water. As odd as this might sound, having time where you're soaking in the higher frequency energy that the natural world provides is vital to maintaining your energy reserves while simultaneously calming your nervous system.

Most people I know who have Master numbers in their charts report a strong need for time outside, unplugged, and away from the static of the technological world.

"YOU'RE GETTING VERY ... VERY ... SLEEPY ..."

You need rest. Not excessively so. Nowhere near as much sleep as you might if you were experiencing depression or an illness. However, you will thrive if you have a stable sleep cycle and take power naps occasionally. Understand that you're running a lot of energy through your body all the time! This can mean that fatigue is a common denominator in your life.

Often folks with Master numbers are also master lucid dreamers. Another reason you may need more rest than others is that you're doing a lot of work in other realms while asleep. During certain periods of your life, you may experience segments of time in which you wake exhausted. It's therefore beneficial to be sensitive to yourself and make modifications to your schedule as necessary. Understand that there are times to accelerate and times to decelerate a bit.

Also, know that there are periods of time where sometimes sleep will elude you because of added stress you're experiencing, or because you have found yourself reaching yet another significant reinvention point. Just know that securing somewhat consistent restorative sleep is necessary to carry you forward with your Master mission.

ET PHONE HOME

Those with Master numbers often feel isolated—whether literally or figuratively. It's always beneficial therefore to widen your perspective and get outside of your head. You can do this in so many ways—such as by reading and learning about whatever might intrigue you in the world of metaphysics. Try surrounding yourself as much as you can with people who are like-minded, so you don't feel alone or abnormal. You may need to seek out these people and actively cultivate these relationships. I find that when many people with Master numbers feel stressed they *disengage*. In actuality, however, this is precisely when they should reach out and seek support.

You're meant for more. You can feel it. You stew about it, grind about it, and angst about it. What qualifies as "more" to you as an individual? *More* can be lifting yourself from a childhood built on abuse, poverty, or any other kind of severe circumstances. It may also mean a host of other things.

I've always been fascinated about this quandary. Some people come from childhoods comprised primarily of despair, abuse, war, violence, drug and alcohol abuse, and other kinds of horrific circumstances that created a harrowing everyday reality for them as children. Some of these people grow up, and through some miracle they defy of the law of averages and end up forging ahead and getting an education, perhaps climbing ranks in their career, getting married or into a healthy partnership, and then having children and being stellar and loving parents. How does this happen when these people had virtually no role models upon which to base their choices and behavior?

And then by the same token, how is it that a person who is privileged overall through ethnicity, education, gender, financial support or security, and an overall supportive upbringing can become the addict, the person who can't cope with life, the lone gunman, or the abusive spouse or parent? How can it be that the person with such a foundation of entitlement can detour into the abyss?

Numerology helped me make sense of this. If you resonate with numerology, you can begin to understand some underlying drivers and stumbling blocks for each of us that may not make sense to you given your outlook on life, yet you can still start to comprehend some of the core issues at work.

If you experience this feeling I'm describing of being meant for more and you have a Master number (or several Master numbers) in your chart, be mindful and widen your lens. Look for signs of your underlying potential. Sometimes a Master calling has little to do with being a billionaire and more to do with creating financial security or moderate abundance in your life, especially if you come from poverty or even from circumstances where money was a trigger point.

This is also viewable from the other side of the fence. Perhaps you were brought up with wealth, yet you could see the personal cost of gaining and maintaining that level of wealth and you made the determination that you didn't want to engage with money in that same way. You didn't want to sell your soul to money as a "god," and you realized somewhere along the line that the way in which this wealth was gained and maintained didn't align with your inherent value system. Your Master calling may have little to do with being famous, being the founder and CEO of a company, or being the inventor of some significant product or service. Sometimes a Master calling has to do with taking yourself from *here* to *there* in a way that is rather profound in one lifetime if you really step back and look at it objectively.

This isn't to say that sometimes the result of your Master efforts manifests as a heightened level of success in the world through business, entertainment, or other avenues where your influence can be far reaching. It *does* mean that you're not a failure if you develop and act upon your Master calling in substantially "smaller" ways—highly targeted or even intimate ways. At the end of the day, it's all about giving back in some way, shape, or form.

Understand that there are times in your Master number life where you are just *so over it!* Most people with Master numbers go through several "just f@*k it" stages. There will be times when you retract, disengage, give up, become angry, defensive, maybe even self-destructive. I find that people with Master numbers can become remarkably disconnected and overwhelmed with feeling distraught about the state of the world or even about their own individual lives. You'll have moments of emotional paralysis or where you can't focus or make decisions about the way you want to focus your attention and your efforts. You'll perhaps long for a more straightforward existence. Or yearn for ease, certainty, and predictability. Those aspects of life rarely find you, and if they do, their attraction is usually short lived. You'll always be called back home—to your true calling—even if it takes some kicking and screaming to get there.

Understand that your Master numbers offer you a reservoir of talent, ability, past-life wisdom, quirky charisma, and high-level spiritual/intuitive ability. *Remember that the energy of the Master number is what is available to you and it's also what drives you.* A central idea to keep in mind as you traverse your Master path is that life is what happens while we're waiting for everything to make sense and fall into place. Because you're destined for an intense ride, more than likely it'll be a rarity for you to feel wholly level and situated. It's a good idea therefore to get used to, and embrace, a certain amount of turbulence. Make friends with uncertainty while also choosing to define a sense of purpose in your everyday engagements, interactions, and experiences.

My yoga teacher shared an essential element for those carrying Master vibrations. He said we could "suffer or soften." A key ingredient for stepping into the Master energy and the directives it brings is to lighten up and truly accept that there is no final destination. Every step is your destination, and how you handle every curveball, crisis, happy surprise, and everything in between is a true test of how you're mastering the aspects of your life that Master numbers put in front of you.

Remember that the 11/2 and the 22/4 share the sensitivity of the number 2. There can be a part of you—as you read the remark that success comes when you "soften"—doing an eye roll right now. You may be wondering how you could possibly soften any more than you already do. Being acutely emotionally sensitive has always been a guiding force, often to what you undoubtedly consider your own detriment. You've worked hard to disengage from your doormat status at certain times in your life. You already feel slightly insecure and emotionally raw.

The trick is to understand the exciting and profound difference between "softness" as the equivalent of being a "pushover" and softness as the equivalent to being "supple" and "resilient." The true nature of softness in this context is the suppleness and the resilience of being adaptable, forgiving, and standing in a posture of non-judgment.

The lesson of the number 2 has to do with the strengthening of emotional boundaries to such a point where the engagement doesn't result in deep hurt, emotional withdrawal, and long-held grudges. Think of it as being like a trampoline: The surface is strong, yet it offers you the ability to jump, bounce, and do aerial summersaults! So, the call to action here is to soften to the point where, like Popeye would say, "I 'yam' what I 'yam,'"—without feeling constant anxiety because you have to prove yourself to the world. Your mastery will come to fruition when you no longer feel the urge or the need to bolster, justify, or assert yourself—or the need to recruit others to your side, point of view, or to acknowledge your greatness. There is no benefit in conquering others. Remember Byron Katie's suggestion that's so apt for the number 2: "Spare yourself from seeking love, approval, or appreciation—from anyone. And watch what happens in reality.

Here are five principles that everyone working with Master numbers must adhere to, and master on some level, to fulfill their destiny.

- *Be altruistic.* Those with Master numbers must actively engage in some selfless service. This is at the core of the calling for the Master numbers.
- *Actively engage with the Twelve Laws of Karma* (see box on page 226).
- *Discipline your emotions.* The path of the Master numbers demands expert engagement with feelings while detaching from emotional entanglements.
- *Step into yourself while also getting over yourself.* Those with Master numbers must regulate their egos, whereby they must empower themselves, yet, at the same time, not elevating themselves as better or more important than other people.
- *Gain true humility.* Humility is defined as freedom from pride or arrogance—the quality or state of being humble.

The core guiding principle for every person with Master numbers is *love.* The energy of the 11/2 resides in learning about, acting with, and accepting love. The Master 22/4 brings a double dose of loving energy to the hard-working ability to make things happen in the world. The strength of the 33/6 resonates with the same power of love and service. The lives of those with Master numbers are measured, as all beings are measured, by how they engage with others, their passion for their work, and how well they have loved.

As someone working with Master numbers, you'll experience intensity in your life that may sometimes feel like torment, and yet the power behind your drive to elevate yourself to your highest and best is all part of the art of actively becoming conscious and bringing your Master mission to fruition. As you find focus, direction, and a level of lighthearted flow, you'll be able to harness and utilize the power and influence that is your birthright. *The gift and purpose are in the doing*—in the day-to-day choices you make and act upon. Aim high and make it count. Trust yourself and surround yourself with support and like-minded people. You have tremendous power to exert positive influence every day and in every way.

THE TWELVE LAWS OF KARMA:
GUIDING PRINCIPLES FOR MASTER NUMBERS 11/2, 22/4, AND 33/6

THE GREAT LAW

What comes around goes around. As you sow, so shall you reap. Whatever we put out into the universe comes back to us. (Also known as the Law of Cause and Effect.)

THE LAW OF CREATION

You attract what you are, not what you want. Be and do yourself what you want to have in your life.

THE LAW OF HUMILITY

What you refuse to accept will continue for you.

THE LAW OF GROWTH

Wherever you go, there you are. To grow you need to change. It is unnecessary to change what is around you.

THE LAW OF RESPONSIBILITY

Whenever there is something wrong, face that there is something wrong with you.

THE LAW OF CONNECTION

Every step is essential, even the ones we think are inconsequential. Everything in the universe interweaves.

THE LAW OF FOCUS

You can't think of two things at the same time.

THE LAW OF GIVING AND HOSPITALITY

If you believe something to be true, then sometime in your life you must demonstrate that truth.

THE LAW OF HERE AND NOW

Looking back at what was prevents us from being entirely present in the here and now. Holding on to the old prevents us from having the new.

THE LAW OF CHANGE

History repeats itself until we learn the lessons that we need to learn to change our path.

THE LAW OF PATIENCE AND REWARD

All rewards require toil. Rewards of lasting value require patient and persistent effort.

THE LAW OF SIGNIFICANCE AND INSPIRATION

You get back from something what you've put into it.

ACKNOWLEDGMENTS

Thank you to my Master number clients who have encouraged the writing of this book.

Thank you to my initial readers: Angie Offstein, Shelly George, Shayna Samuels, Jennifer Hope Sweitzer, Suzanne Kvilhaug, Nancy McCleary, and Elizabeth Joy Mueller.

As always, my thanks to Miranda and Phoebe for your continued love, support, and laughter.

END NOTES

Chapter 2: Core Elements of Numerology

1. Juno Jordan. *Numerology: The Romance in Your Name* (Camarillo, CA.: DeVorss & Company, 1984), p. 110.
2. Hans Decoz. "Numerology and the Letter Y," WorldNumerology.com (accessed February 26, 2018), https://www.worldnumerology.com/numerology-Y-vowel-consonant.htm.

Chapter 4: Your Name and Master Numbers

1. His Holiness Pope Francis. "Why the Only Future Worth Building Includes Everyone," TED.com (April 2017), http://www.ted.com/talks/pope_francis_why_the_only_future_worth_building_includes_everyone.
2. Matthew Oliver Goodwin. *Numerology: The Complete Guide—Volume One* (Franklin Lakes, N.J.: New Page Books,1982), p. 78.

Chapter 6: The Master Number 11/2

1. Faith Javane. *Master Numbers: Cycles of Divine Order* (Atglen, PA.: Schiffer Publishing, 1997), p. 81.
2. Matthew Oliver Goodwin. *Numerology: The Complete Guide—Volume One* (Franklin Lakes, N.J.: New Page Books,1982),
3. Juno Jordan. *The Romance in Your Name* (Camarillo, CA.: DeVorss & Company, 1984), p. 65.
4. Javane, p. 82.
5. Goodwin, p. 78.
6. Hans Decoz with Tom Monte. *Numerology: A Complete Guide to Understanding and Using Your Numbers of Destiny—Key to Your Inner Self* (New York: Avery Publishing Group, 1994), p. 32.
7. Ibid.
8. Ibid.
9. "Stephen Colbert on Building Community Through *The Late Show*," Super Soul Sessions [Video] (March 2018). Available at: http://www.oprah.com/own-supersoulsessions/stephen-colbert-on-building-community-through-the-the-late-show.

10. Ibid.
11. Ibid.

Chapter 10: The Flipside of Number 2
1. Byron Katie. Visit her website: http://thework.com/en.

Chapter 11: Bringing the Double 1 into the 2
1. Dan Millman. *The Life You Were Born to Live: A Guide to Finding Your Life Purpose* (Novato, CA.: New World Library, 1993), p. 136.

Chapter 13: Five Ways to Understand and Integrate the Master 11/2
1. "Living Brave with Brené Brown and Oprah Winfrey," YouTube.com (posted June 13, 2016) [VIDEO]. Available at: https://www.youtube.com/watch?v=4u4J58YUB1Q.

Chapter 15: Master Number 22/4
1. Dan Millman. *The Life You Were Born to Live: A Guide to Finding Your Life Path* (New York: H.J. Kramer, 1992), p. 196.

Chapter 16: Number 4
1. Kay Lagerquist and Lisa Lenard. *The Complete Idiot's Guide to Numerology: Release the Power of Spiritual Numerology in Your Life, Second Edition* (New York: Alpha Books, 2009), p. 130.

Chapter 18: Bringing the Double 2 into the 4
1. Dan Millman. *The Life You Were Born to Live: A Guide to Finding Your Life Purpose* (Novato, CA.: New World Library, 1993), p. 199.
2. Ibid, p. 196.
3. Kay Lagerquist and Lisa Lenard. *The Complete Idiot's Guide to Numerology: Release the Power of Spiritual Numerology in Your Life, Second Edition* (New York: Alpha Books, 2009), p. 123.
4. Juno Jordan. *The Romance in Your Name* (Camarillo, CA.: DeVorss & Company, 1984), p. 66.
5. Millman, pp. 197–8.

Chapter 19: The Challenges of the Master 22/4

1. Kristen Bell, from a Twitter interview. YouTube.com (posted September 8, 2017). Available at: https://www.youtube.com/watch?v=XXhk448-GAQ.

Chapter 21: Master Number 33/6

1. Dan Millman. *The Life You Were Born to Live: A Guide to Finding Your Life Purpose* (Novato, CA.: New World Library, 1993), p. 237.
2. Hans Decoz. "Numerology Course Part 1," WorldNumerology.com Available at: https://www.worldnumerology.com/numerology-Course-01.htm.
3. Faith Javane. *Master Numbers: Cycles of Divine Order* (Atglen, PA.: Whitford Press, 1988), p. 94.
4. Peter Dinklage. "The Best Commencement Speeches, Ever," NPR.org. Available at: http://apps.npr.org/commencement/speech/peter-dinklage-bennington-college-2012.

Chapter 25: The Flipside of Number 6

1. Martha Beck. "How to Stop Being a Martyr," Oprah.com (accessed April 5, 2018). Available at: http://www.oprah.com/inspiration/how-to-stop-being-a-martyr.

Chapter 26: Bringing the Double 3 into the 6

1. Dan Millman. *The Life You Were Born to Live: A Guide to Finding Your Life Path* (New York: H.J. Kramer, 1992), p. 237.
2. Meryl Streep (2010). "The Best Commencement Speeches, Ever," NPR.org. Available at: https://apps.npr.org/commencement/speech/meryl-streep-barnard-college-2010.
3. Millman, p. 238.
4. Kay Lagerquist and Lisa Lenard. *The Complete Idiot's Guide to Numerology: Release the Power of Spiritual Numerology in Your Life, Second Edition* (New York: Alpha Books, 2009), p. 132–3.
5. Henry Seltzer. Visit his website: https://astrograph.com/horoscopes.php.
6. Millman, p. 236.

Chapter 35: Observations on Master Numbers

1. Stephanie Eckhardt. "A Beautiful, Bewitching Conversation with Jim Carrey, Who Has Returned Reborn," WMagazine.com (September 22, 2017). Available at: https://www.wmagazine.com/story/jim-carrey-michel-gondry-show-art-exhibit.

2. Esther Hicks. Visit her website: https://aaa.abraham-hicks.com.

3. Jeff Foster and Nic Higham. "The Perfect Balance of Acceptance and Rejection," YouTube.com [Video] (December 15, 2011). Available at: https://www.youtube.com/watch?v=3j_ZYSRR2p0.

4. Alan Watts and David Lindberg. "Why Your Life Is Not a Journey," BeFreeToday.com (accessed April 5, 2018). Available at: http://www.befreetoday.com.au/alan-watts-life-not-journey.

5. Anthony Robbins (posted January 31, 2018). Source: https://www.facebook.com/TonyRobbins/posts/10156267068244060.

6. Adyashanti. Source: https://www.goodreads.com/quotes/378539-enlightenment-is-a-destructive-process-it-has-nothing-to-do.

7. Oprah Winfrey. Visit her website: https://oprah.com.

SELECT BIBLIOGRAPHY

Avery, Kevin Quinn. *The Numbers of Life: The Hidden Power in Numerology* (Girard & Stewart, 1977).

Brill, Michael. *Numerology for Decoding Behavior: Your Personal Numbers at Work, with Family, and in Relationships* (Rochester, VT.: Destiny Books, 2011).

Decoz, Hans with Tom Monte. *Numerology: A Complete Guide to Understanding and Using Your Numbers of Destiny—Key to Your Inner Self* (New York: Avery Publishing Group, 1994).

Fairchild, Alana. *Messages in the Numbers: The Universe Is Talking to You* (Woodbury, MN.: Llewellyn Publications, 2015).

Goodwin, Matthew Oliver. *Numerology: The Complete Guide—Volume One* (Franklin Lakes, N.J.: New Page Books, 1981).

Javane, Faith. *Master Numbers: Cycles of Divine Order* (Atglen, PA.: Whitford Press, 1988).

Jordan, Juno. *Your Right Action Number: Learn How Numerology Can Help You Make Career, Relationship, and Financial Decisions* (Marina del Rey, CA.: DeVorss & Company, 1979).

Jordan, Juno. *Numerology: The Romance in Your Name* (Marina del Rey, CA.: DeVorss & Company, 1965).

Jordan, Juno and Helen Houston. *Your Name, Your Number, Your Destiny: Two Guides to Numerology* (North Hollywood, CA.: Newcastle Publishing, 1982).

Kirkman, Patricia and Katherine A. Gleason. *The Complete Idiot's Guide: Numerology Workbook* (New York: Alpha Books, 2004).

Lagerquist, Kay and Lisa Lenard. *The Complete Idiot's Guide to Numerology: Release the Power of Spiritual Numerology in Your Life, Second Edition* (New York: Alpha Books, 2009).

Line, Julia. *The Numerology Workbook: Understanding and Using the Power of Numbers* (New York: Sterling Publishing, 1985).

McCants, Glynis. *Glynis Has Your Number: Discover What Life Has in Store for You Through the Power of Numerology* (New York: Hyperion, 2005).

Millman, Dan. *The Life You Were Born to Live: A Guide to Finding Your Life Purpose* (Novato, CA.: New World Library, 1993).

Phillips, David A. *The Complete Book of Numerology: Discovering the Inner Self* (Encinitas, CA.: Hay House, 1992).

Strayhorn, Lloyd. *Numbers and You: A Numerology Guide for Everyday Living* (New York: Ballantine Books, 1997).

ABOUT THE AUTHOR

Felicia Bender, Ph.D., is the author of *Redesign Your Life: Using Numerology to Create the Wildly Optimal You*. She earned a doctorate in theater from the University of Missouri–Columbia. Felicia is passionate about writing, counseling, teaching, and presenting ways to use numerology, spirituality, and intuition to understand ourselves and others on a deep level—to validate our life purpose and to develop tools to understand how to trust our own intuitive language. A contributor to ElephantJournal.com, Numerologist.com, and other media, she is the resident numerologist for AstroStyle.com and you can find her at FeliciaBender.com.

Printed in Great Britain
by Amazon

80830354R00139